LAND, FAITH, AND VOICE

Jenny Stanford Series on Sacred Music *Vol. I*

LAND, FAITH, AND VOICE
Christian Music in the Pacific Northwest

Alexander Rosenblatt

JENNY STANFORD
PUBLISHING

Published by

Jenny Stanford Publishing Pte. Ltd.
101 Thomson Road
#06-01, United Square
Singapore 307591

Email: editorial@jennystanford.com
Web: www.jennystanford.com

British Library Cataloguing-in-Publication Data
A catalogue record for this book is available from the British Library.

Land, Faith, and Voice: Christian Music in the Pacific Northwest

ISBN 978-981-5129-11-3 (Hardcover)
ISBN 978-1-003-47332-9 (eBook)

To my son Yehonatan, who showed great interest in this research and helped me find relevant sites and ethnography during my four trips to the Pacific Northwest.

Contents

Preface

The idea of this book finally crystallized in February 2021, during the pandemic lockdown, when two circumstances made it possible to think about a book, rather than an article on this topic. The first such issue was a grant I received from my home institution for a trip to the Pacific Northwest, and the second was the decision of the Centre for Studies in Religion and Society (CSRS) at the University of Victoria to implement my visiting position, scheduled for the summer of 2021, remotely, following the new technical opportunities provided to us in this period.

Traveling to Greater Vancouver and Victoria (BC), Seattle and Vancouver (WA), and Portland (OR) in 2021 and 2022 gave me new geographic and sociocultural perspectives for comparison, whereas the approach to the University of Victoria library, the friendly attitude of the library staff who are always ready to help, and, of course, fruitful discussions with CSRS visiting fellows and staff during the weekly meetings on Zoom expanded the original scope of the topic, making it relevant to the book.

I would like to acknowledge:

- The Halbert Center for Canadian Studies at the Hebrew University of Jerusalem for awarding me the Arie Shachar Postdoctoral Fellowship in Canadian Studies (2013);
- The University of British Columbia School of Music and personally Prof. Michael Tenzer, ethnomusicologist, for hosting and mentoring my postdoctoral project and for the travel grant to present on this topic at an interdisciplinary conference on the Harvard campus (2014);
- The Centre for Studies in Religion and Society at the University of Victoria, British Columbia, Canada, for invitation as a visiting research fellow (2021);
- The Research Authority of Zefat Academic College, Israel, for providing me with a research grant to collect ethnography in the Pacific Northwest (2021).

So far, presentations on topics related to this book have been made at the University of British Columbia (the School of Music and St. John's College); meeting of the council of parishioners of St. James' Anglican Church in Greater Vancouver; the IJAS conference on the Harvard Campus (all in 2014); and the 46th World Conference of the International Council for Traditional Music, Lisbon (2022).

Alexander Rosenblatt

Autumn 2023

Introduction

The border crossing is behind, and immediately the road sign "60," indicating the speed limit in miles. My son is smiling: "Imperial miles! The most advanced country in the world seems to never go metric! How many yards is a mile, by the way?" We have just crossed the Canada–U.S. border with a rented Toyota. As guests in both these countries, we are required to pass an interview with the border officer. My UBC (University of British Columbia) Faculty card helps to shorten the process once we approach the counter. This is my second visit to the region after the postdoctoral academic year in Vancouver several years back. I liked so much the greatness of the Northwest Nature, the ranges of mountains, universal tranquility, and the benevolence of the people, that I decided at the first opportunity to come here with my son.

The first such opportunity came in the summer of 2017. We arrived in Vancouver and settled in a university dorm, right across from the St. John's residential college where I lived during my postdoctoral period. We did not even have to rent a car until the very last day, as public transportation in Greater Vancouver is very convenient, combining buses, trolleybuses, and light rail, which is controlled by a computer system without operators. At first, it looks strange, even frightening, but when you find out that this system has been working like this for 35 (!) years without a single emergency, you calm down and take a closer look at the carriages of this miraculous transport. And yet there is something to see! Clean, tidy cars running an energy-saving program returning electricity to the grid when braking. And the inscription on each car: "British Columbia. The Best Place on Earth" next to the logo: the sun, rising from behind a range of mountains. This transport is named SkyTrain, since it is only in the center of the city underground, and otherwise on poles, without occupying the area of the roadway.

There is a striking variety of cultural wealth that draw visitors to the region, along with the industrial and high-tech industries, world trade enterprises, and top-brand coffee shops. Thus, for example,

Greater Seattle has the biggest in the world facility for building Boeing airplanes (there are factory tours for visitors), as well as the headquarters of such giants as Microsoft, Amazon, and Starbucks. Space Needle, the 180-meter lookout tower, during the construction of which no one was hurt as the billboards state, has long become a symbol of the city.

However, the main purpose of each of my trips to this region was collecting ethnography on church music practiced today in various churches of Victoria and Greater Vancouver (BC), Seattle and Vancouver (WA), and Portland (OR), that is, the area commonly referred to as the Pacific Northwest. This book summarizes a decade of research on this topic, while each specific perspective either formed in advance or arose in the process of ethnography and its analysis. The book explores various aspects of Christian music in British Columbia, Washington, and Oregon, but primarily its historical facets and local palette. The scope of the main topics covers aspects such as historical and local melodies in relevant hymnbooks, musical practices in the cathedrals and other churches within the designated area, and the creative profile of modern North American composers (including those who have worked in the Pacific Northwest), who made significant contributions to the church music practiced in the area. Other background and supporting topics are a brief reference to the history and culture of the Canadian and U.S. parts of the region, the study of native Christian art, its philosophy and examples, and historical stages and the current landscape of Christianity in British Columbia, Washington State, and Oregon.

The book aims to prove that musical practices in churches of different denominations throughout the region have much in common, whether it is an emphasis on the historical heritage of traditions, a global approach to music selection in hymnbooks and church services, or a tribute to local melodies and customs in both liturgical and paraliturgical events. The point to be argued is that post-missionary churches, even more so than missionary ones, preserve the historical background of their churches, and at the same time, they are much more sensitive and respectful of the ethnic traditions and music (and even the customs of the original religious affiliation) of their parishes. The book aims to provide an overview of the historical and sociocultural layers of the religious tradition, which, diverse in itself, unites the inhabitants of this area, who come from different ethnic and cultural backgrounds—descendants of British (and European continental) settlers, newcomers from Asian and some other countries as well as those who have lived here since time immemorial.

The familiarization with the subject began in the framework of my postdoctoral project "Music of the Contemporary Anglican Churches in Greater Vancouver: Outlines of Cultural Diversity" carried out at the School of Music, UBC in 2013–2014. It was an ethnographic study in nine Anglican churches of Greater Vancouver with different ethnic backgrounds. About 30 audio recordings of liturgical and paraliturgical events in these churches, associated with three separate Anglican institutions (after the church split in the middle of the first decade of the century), provided me with extensive field material. This ethnography was continued with additional information: interviews with clergy, musicians, and community members, printed copies of hymnbooks used in each of these churches, church leaflets and booklets as well as photocopies of historical Canadian hymnbooks and materials about Healey Willan (1880–1968), a distinguished (albeit little-known outside of Canada) British-Canadian composer who has made a major contribution to the way music sounds today in the modern Canadian church. Later on, while traveling with my son to Vancouver (BC), Seattle, and the UK (2017, 2018, and 2019, respectively), I found myself continuing to collect relevant information and attend church services and other relevant events in each of the above places. In 2021, I was (remotely) enrolled as a visiting researcher at the Centre for Study of Religion and Society (CSRS), University of Victoria (BC). In parallel, I received a research grant from my home institution Zefat Academic College (Israel) for a trip to Seattle (August–September 2021). Finally, in August 2022, I traveled with my son to Victoria (BC) and Portland (OR) to complete the collection of ethnography for this project.

The book is intended for scientists and students involved in the broad spectrum of social studies and humanities. The relevant chapters collect considerations about traditionalism, the ritual and artistic aspects of worship, and an innovative approach that, in turn, takes into account global trends and carefully searches for the appropriate use of local motives. Other parts of the book describe the wisdom and unique approach of the Native art to the symbols of the Christian faith. Summing up the results of ethnomusicological (at its core) study, the book touches on related areas of research that make it relevant for scientists involved in anthropology, sociology, religious studies, cultural studies, musicology, art, and some other disciplines. The study began at a time when ethnographic research involved fieldwork, contacting "informants," and reference to their interpretation of various issues related to the phenomenon under study. In the course of the study, however, the situation began to change, and by the final stage, the pandemic forced many research industries to switch to online forms of obtaining information, which was not available in the old days, when information could be accessed only through communication with its carriers. I was lucky enough to use both methods in one (not even really longitudinal) study.

The scientific perspective chosen for this book can be defined as music as a mirror of church ministry; church ministry as a mirror of public life; all while reflecting on the idyllic nature of the Pacific Northwest and the ability of people of different ethnic and cultural backgrounds to show mutual interest and respect. The range of books with a similar perspective may include Appadurai's study of modernity [1]. This book, however, does not correspond to any certain locality and its inhabitants in terms of ethnographic research. Browner [2] presents an approach to the music of a wide group of indigenous people in North America, namely the First Nations. However, social and spiritual divides are far from the topic of this book. Donaldson [3] analyses the hymnbooks of the Protestant churches in the United States and Canada throughout their history for motives associated with indigenous and global origins. Perry [4] provides comprehensive information on the architectural and interior design of indigenous churches in British Columbia, with a description of the history of the communities involved. This book, while not an academic monograph, is a very valuable source of knowledge about local Christianity in the Canadian Pacific Northwest. Bruce-Mitford [5] shares her knowledge of the signs and symbols of various cultures and periods. This cross-cultural monograph, focused on its subject through reference to the sociocultural context, is somewhat similar to the current book, although it is designed more as a guide to physical and graphic objects endowed with semantic meaning. The final book to be listed here is Nerburn [6], an edited volume of thoughtful writings by respected Native American leaders and thinkers. Collected and categorized for use by a wider English-speaking audience, this information provides examples of indigenous knowledge presented in the context of both traditional and modern life.

The summary below serves to navigate between the parts and chapters of the book.

PART I: LAND, FAITH, AND ART

This part of three chapters introduces the reader to the history of one of the most beautiful places on the planet and its Christian institutions, as well as unique examples of indigenous peoples' understanding of Christian concepts and symbols.

Chapter 1. Pacific Northwest: Land, People, and Culture

The purpose of this chapter is to provide an objective historical, demographic, and cultural picture of the region. While the history of European settlement in the Pacific coastal region of what is now Canada and the U.S. is important to this chapter, it focuses mainly on the attractiveness of this fertile land with a mild climate for those who have lived here since time immemorial, for the settlers of the past three centuries and for those who immigrated here in the late 20th – early 21st century. All this corpus of demographic groups with their languages, cultural attributes, religion, and customs is unique to this entire locality, which itself differs from place to place within this region.

Chapter 2. Christianity in British Columbia, Washington, and Oregon

This chapter provides a historical perspective and current panorama of Christian institutions and communities in the Canadian and American Pacific Northwest. The topics include: (a) the historical stages of the baseline and missionary churches; (b) statistics on hymnbooks, denominations, and churches, including heritage churches of indigenous peoples; and (c) the current agenda, philosophy, and approaches to traditional and sensitive issues.

Arguments for expanding the Christian worldview in the area list the inclusion of native customs and practices on the agenda of church services in Greater Vancouver, elements of the Far-Eastern practices in Portland, and the Celtic Eucharist and Litany of Reconciliation with the one-bell ring in Victoria.

Chapter 3. Native Christian Art: Philosophy and Examples

This chapter reveals the philosophy and visual manifestations of indigenous peoples in relation to Christianity. Part of this continuum is how respected indigenous leaders share their wisdom and worldviews. Another point is what the church fathers think about native Christians and their wisdom, and what native Christians say about themselves and their views on Christianity. Another part of the discussion is reflections on the visual concepts of Christian plots presented in native Christian art. These samples will be compared with other examples of traditional and modern native art. A discussion of the interiors and exteriors of indigenous churches complements the themes of the chapter.

PART II: MUSIC IN THE CHURCH

This part aims to delineate what makes the church service in the Pacific Northwest so discernible. Three chapters discuss the three main components of the musical part of the ministry and paraliturgical activities, which is actually the most visible factor in this distinction.

Chapter 4. Historical and Local Tunes in Hymnbooks

Most of the churches in the area, primarily those associated with the Western Church, use hymnbooks published with music, so visitors who hold such a book and see the hymn numbers on the hymn board can easily join congregational singing. In most churches, hymnbooks have become the only prescribed source for congregational singing. That is why the compilation of these books (every two or three decades) has become an event and an important message to society from the church fathers. Legacy and historical depth of the musical tradition of the Western Church (considering the differences in approaches to the subject, characteristic of the Catholic and Protestant churches), contemporary sacred songs, melodies representing different musical cultures around the world, and finally, local folk melodies—this is a cultural and historical message in the hymnbooks used in a particular church. The study showed that different sociocultural agenda of clergypersons in the same denomination led to the use of different hymnbooks for ministry in their churches.

Chapter 5. Musical Practices in Cathedrals and Parish Churches

The musical patterns of worship in churches of even one denomination can vary greatly depending on the musical milieu of the parishioners of a particular church and the personal preferences of the community leader (clergyperson). Paraliturgical and other cultural events in a particular church can also be carried out in a traditional way, or alternatively, in a modern or local way. Examples of how cathedrals and parish churches in British Columbia, Washington, and Oregon support different musical frameworks are the subject of this chapter. Thus, church music festivals, weekly Evensong, Taizé music, indigenous songs, a children's choir singing in different languages, and a professional choir performing a wide repertoire in the churches of Greater Vancouver and Victoria (BC), Seattle and Vancouver (WA), and Portland (OR) will be discussed along with the musical portion of the regular Eucharistic service.

Chapter 6. Contribution of Modern Composers to the Church Music in the Region

Local composers have always contributed to church services, first in their regions and then in other parts of the world. North American composers of the twentieth century were no exception: their compositions in the genres of church music, primarily for collective singing, can be found in hymnbooks of the national churches of Canada and the U.S. For example, Healey Willan, a British-born Canadian composer, made a great contribution to the revival of plainsongs (modal tunes associated with medieval style) and wrote many choral and organ compositions, performed mainly in Canadian churches. Other composers and musicians, including current and former residents of the Pacific Northwest, such as Patrick Wedd, Rupert Lang, and others, have contributed or are contributing to the musical portion of church services by composing and performing music related to the musical cultures of worshippers in churches of the region in which they act as organists and choirmasters. This chapter is devoted to the musical portraits of these composers.

Part I
LAND, FAITH, AND ART

Chapter 1

Pacific Northwest: Land, People, and Culture

Which came first, the chicken or the egg? Canada or USA? British Columbia or Christopher Columbus? When and what exactly did Columbus discover? If he discovered what is now called British Columbia, then why is it "British" and Columbus seems to have been Spanish or Italian? And why are Montreal and Quebec considered the oldest cities on the continent founded by Europeans, if they are far from the coast, where Columbus, who simply thought he found a shortcut to India, could arrive?

The very last question to ask here is how did we all live before Wikipedia and Google Maps?

Revisiting the Discovery

The quick reference below is aimed at refreshing a history of European discoveries and settlements in the Americas.

It is generally accepted that the "discovery of America" belongs to Columbus. Well, this is only partly true, since the Italian explorer and navigator Cristoforo Colombo (1451–1506), better known as

Land, Faith, and Voice: Christian Music in the Pacific Northwest
Alexander Rosenblatt
Copyright © 2024 Jenny Stanford Publishing Pte. Ltd.
ISBN 978-981-5129-11-3 (Hardcover), 978-1-003-47332-9 (eBook)
www.jennystanford.com

Christopher Columbus (Fig. 1), never set foot in North America. Over the course of four separate voyages, the first of which began in 1492, Columbus reached various Caribbean islands that are now the Bahamas and the island later named Hispaniola. He also explored the coasts of Central and South America. But he did not reach the North American continent, which was already inhabited by the local peoples, moreover, he never thought he had found a new continent [7].

Figure 1. Columbus in an engraving by Nicolas de Larmessin, 1682. New York Public Library.

The pioneer of the "way to Canada" was the French sailor Jacques Cartier (1491–1557), the first European to travel inland in North America. He was sent by the French King François I to the New World in search of gold. He was also instructed to find a sea passage to Asia. In 1534, Jacques Cartier explored and mapped the Gulf of St. Lawrence. In 1535, on three ships, he went up the St. Lawrence River to Stadacona, the Indian village where the city of Quebec is now located. The French entered into negotiations with the local Iroquois Indians led by Chief Donnacona and declared the surrounding lands the possession of the French king, giving them the name *Canada*— from the Iroquois word *Kanata*, which meant many huts, or simply "village" [8, p. 7].

Over the following two hundred years, the relationships between the newcomers and locals in the inner part of the continent—present Illinois and Michigan—were such that one day in 1725, French settlers in Illinois sent Chief Agapit Chicagou of the *Mitchigamea* and five other chiefs to Paris. The immediate purpose of this gesture was to meet the leaders of the indigenous peoples with King Louis XV and present him with a letter of allegiance to the French crown. This historical fact clearly shows that the French presence in the region prevailed over other European or British presences in the early 18th century. And yet, what else do we know about this delegation in Paris? Studies of the early 20th century, based on historical letters, indicate that the chiefs, while presented to King Louis XV, were dressed "in savage costume" [9, p. 289]. Moreover, they most likely demonstrated their traditional dances in front of the king and his retinue, inspiring the court composer Jean-Philippe Rameau (1683–1764) to compose, 10 years later, his famous rondeau *Les Sauvages*, the most impressive part of his opera-ballet *Les Indes galantes*. Itself, the fact that the early 18th century composer writes a musical-stage work on the love topic in exotic (for the European eyes of that time) places—The Ottoman Empire, Peru, Persia, and North America— deserves attention as a rather unique phenomenon in its kind.

But back to the North American perspective, to the area of interest to us—the Pacific Northwest.

Settlement on the Northwest Coast

First of all, we define the terms that will be used in what follows. Under the name Pacific Northwest, three neighboring territories will be considered (from north to south)—Canadian British Columbia and two U.S. states—Washington and Oregon. It is these territories that are commonly referred to as the Pacific Northwest, although various sources list under this name several other states and provinces adjacent to the above, namely coastal southern Alaska, as well as Idaho and Yukon, which are landlocked and share to a lesser extent the common features of the "Pacific Northwest."

Who has lived here for thousands of years and why was this region so attractive to live in? Research in recent decades shows that various indigenous peoples have lived along the west coastline for millennia. The Pacific coast is considered as the main migration route for the settlement of America by the peoples of the Late Ice Age who migrated here from northeast Asia [10]. Prehistoric evidence aside, there is an ocean current called the North Pacific Current that moves warmer water along the coast of the Pacific Northwest. This current has a moderating effect on temperatures in West Coast cities such as Vancouver, Seattle, and Portland. Generally, the North Pacific coast is warmer in winter and cooler in summer. About a hundred miles east of these coastal regions, temperatures are much cooler in winter and hotter in summer. The eastern regions also receive much less rainfall than the coastal regions.

The mild and comfortable climate attracted people of different origins and lifestyles to these places, ranging from traditional indigenous tribes to Europeans who brought industry and agriculture here.

Who are the Places Named After

Although the earliest record of European navigations in the region is from the British sailor Francis Drake, who sailed north along the West Coast of North America to Oregon in 1579, the first expedition to reach the northern Pacific Northwest was that of Captain James Cook, who in 1778 reached the [Vancouver] island, just a few months before his unsuccessful trip to Hawaii, where he met his death that gave rise to so many mysteries [11]. However, exploration of the Northwest coast is primarily associated with another British voyager and Royal Navy officer, George Vancouver, who was with Cook on that voyage and returned there 14 years later, in 1792 to explore the island later named after him, along with two towns on the mainland.

The Fraser River, which flows throughout British Columbia, originating in mountains near the border with Alberta and emptying into the Strait of Georgia in the south of Greater Vancouver, near the border with the United States, is named after another traveler, Simon Fraser, who completely traced the river in 1808 and confirmed that it is not connected to the Columbia River. Fraser's name is also given to the second largest university in the province after the University of British Columbia—Simon Fraser University, located in Burnaby, Surrey, and Vancouver cities (all—Greater Vancouver area).

The region also commemorates the leaders of the two nations after whom the city and state are named, namely Victoria, Queen of Great Britain and Ireland, and George Washington, the first president of the United States. Last but not least on this list is Chief Seattle, a respected local leader after whom one of the region's central cities is named. The following is relevant information about the people, whose names are given to territories and urban settlements.

George Vancouver

George Vancouver (1757–1798) was a very famous officer and navigator in the British Royal Navy who managed to complete a number of investigative missions both in North America and elsewhere in the world. His legacy is remembered today by several places bearing his name, primarily the Canadian island and city of Vancouver, the American city of Vancouver, Washington State, and two lesser-known mountains—one in southeast Alaska, on the Yukon border, and the second—near the western coast of the South Island of New Zealand.

Captain George Vancouver (Fig. 2) is most likely a descendant of the Van Coevorden family, possibly the oldest in the Netherlands, meaning "from Coevorden." The municipality of this city traces the lineage of this family back to the 12th century. The grandfather of the future navigator, Lucas Hendrick van Coevorden, anglicized his name to Luke Henry Vancouver after immigrating to England, following the common practice of anglicizing Dutch names [12, 13].

The most significant expedition of Captain Vancouver began in 1791 when he was commissioned to explore the Pacific region. He visited Australia, Zealand, Tahiti, and China, after which he crossed the Pacific Ocean to the coast of modern-day Oregon, from where he continued sailing north. He explored most of the territory of northwestern America. Among the most famous places he visited were Burrard Inlet (the main harbor of the modern city of Vancouver) and the Columbia River.

Figure 2. Anonymous. [Probably] George Vancouver, c. 1796–98. National Portrait Gallery, London.

In 1793, George Vancouver continued his explorations of the northern coast of British Columbia, reaching most of the islands located in the Strait of Georgia, named so by the captain in honor of the then-reigning King George III—not to be confused with the American state of Georgia, formerly named after the grandfather of the king (and his predecessor on the throne), the late King George II.

One of the great explorers of the world completed his work when he was about 40 years old. Yet Vancouver's final years were not happy. He had tuberculosis and was very sick. In addition, during his last voyage, he considered it necessary to punish the young sailor for disobedience, and upon returning home it turned out that the sailor had inherited the noble title. Unfortunately, this newly-made nobleman proved to be mentally unbalanced and spread evil gossip against the captain, who as a result was ridiculed even in his hometown [13]. Be that as it may, Captain George Vancouver remains a central figure in the development of the Pacific Northwest in terms of benefit to sailors and land explorers seeking a temperate climate and safe harbors for the development of international, in particular fur, trade.

Queen Victoria

Victoria (full name: Alexandrina Victoria, 1819–1901) was queen of the United Kingdom of Great Britain and Ireland from 1837 until her death. The future queen was born at Kensington Palace in 1819, and she was fifth in line to the throne. Circumstances developed so that the succession of deaths among her relatives led her to the throne at the age of 18.

The young queen had an outstanding artistic taste and was herself an advanced amateur artist (see Fig. 3) when she married her cousin Albert of the Saxon royal family, who made a reputation for public causes such as the abolition of slavery throughout the world, and he is also credited with introducing the principle that the British royal family should remain above politics [14]. Albert and Victoria collected thousands of works of art that formed the core of the fine art collection now on display at the Victoria and Albert Museum, London, the world's largest museum of applied arts, decorative arts, and design, based on the Great Exhibition of 1851 in the organization of which the prince was personally involved.

Figure 3. Self-portrait sketch by Princess Victoria, 1835, as reproduced in E. Longford, Victoria R.I., London: Weidenfeld & Nicolson, 1964, p. 96.

After the untimely death of her husband in 1861, the widowed queen wore black mourning clothes (the image with which she is usually associated) for the rest of her days and, after a period when she avoided appearing in public, she took up state affairs, although it was a kind of "personal monarchy" in an era when politics in the kingdom was already determined by political parties. Queen Victoria gave birth to eight children and had 42 grandchildren, most of whom had married into Europe's royal families, granting the queen the nickname "Grandmother of Europe."

Queen Victoria's reign has spanned over 63 years, longer than any previous British monarch, surpassed only by her great-great-granddaughter, Queen Elizabeth II, who has been in power for over 70 years (the longest verified reign of any female head of state in history). Known as the Victorian era, this was a period of industrial, political, scientific, and military change in the United Kingdom, marked by a significant expansion of the British Empire, including Vancouver Island in the Pacific Northwest, which became a British Crown Colony in 1849 with Fort Victoria in the southeast as its capital. New settlers arrived, and a small village arose near the fort, which in 1852 became a settlement, named Victoria in honor of the queen [15].

George Washington

The founding father of the United States and the country's first president, George Washington (1732–1799), was a descendant of a once wealthy British family who was granted land by King Henry VIII but lost it during the reign of Oliver Cromwell, after which the grandfather of the future president, Lawrence Washington, migrated to Virginia.

Raised on an agricultural farm and later the owner of one of the largest plantations in Virginia, Washington from a young age was marked by remarkable organizational skills and charisma. It so happened that this man was in the midst of events of historical significance, having made a military career, first in the service of British military units that fought the French Royal Army in Virginia, and then leading the local Continental Army as its commander-in-chief, becoming an American national hero, a central figure in the struggle for independence. During the presidential election of 1789, he won the full vote in the Electoral College, becoming the only president in American history to be elected unanimously.

A look at the portrait (Fig. 4) reveals a problem that has plagued the president from a young age: Washington's teeth have been a mess all his life. He lost his first tooth at the age of 24. At the age of 57, when he was sworn in as president, he had only one tooth left. Numerous dentures, made of different materials, which allowed to maintain a representative image, delivered enormous inconvenience to their wearer, visible in almost every portrait, including the famous portrait on a dollar bill. The president's personal dentist, John Greenwood, preserved his last tooth in a gold locket he wore on his watch fob.

Figure 4. Gilbert Stuart. Portrait of George Washington, 1795. Metropolitan Museum of Art.

As the first president, Washington was well aware that his presidency would set a precedent for all subsequent ones. He carefully carried out the duties and responsibilities of his office, keeping vigilant not to emulate any European royal court. To this end, he preferred the title "Mr. President" to the more impressive names that were offered for this position. He initially turned down a $25,000 salary as he was already wealthy and wanted to protect his image as a dedicated public servant. However, he was persuaded by Congress to accept the compensation so as not to give the impression that only wealthy people could hold the presidency [16].

Chief Seattle

Seattle (or Si'ahl in the traditional Duwamish spelling, c. 1786–1866) was a chief of the Suquamish and Duwamish tribes and a descendant of both of these tribes through his parents (Fig. 5). His father was a Suquamish chief. "Despite an attribution of slavery in his lineage, Seattle's noble status was affirmed by his reception of Thunderbird power from an important supernatural wealth-giver during a vision quest held sometime during his youth" [17]. When the future chief was still a child, he witnessed the arrival of a British ship under the command of Vancouver, anchored off Bainbridge Island in 1792, and happy memories of this visit and his appreciation of the strength and abilities of Westerners remained with him for life.

Seattle's early years as a chief were far from being the peaceful leader of his people. On the contrary, he was described as rather powerful and formidable. However, when his son was killed in a civil strife between the local tribes, the chief was so deeply affected that received baptism into the Catholic Church. His children were also baptized and raised in the faith. Chief Seattle's conversion marked his emergence as a leader seeking cooperation with the incoming American settlers. Seattle's warm welcome and assistance to those who visited his homeland from about 1848 earned him a reputation as a friend of the white people. Since then, Seattle has actively sought out settlers with whom he could do business and trade. He organized a joint fishery, first in Elliott Bay (1851), and a year later in Dzidzulalich, a native village on the eastern shore of the bay. In 1952, a hybrid settlement appeared, named Seattle in honor of the chief.

Chief Seattle's position as an intermediary between the locals and the white settlers was vulnerable. The whites expected him to help them acquire land from the locals. The locals expected him to protect them from white claims. At a certain stage, the whites allocated territory (reservation) for the Suquamish tribe, but not for the Duwamish tribe. From that moment on, Seattle's reputation and influence among the locals went downhill. The leadership of the local Catholic community in Suquamish passed to another local leader.

Figure 5. Chief Seattle. Drawing by R. Coombs (1891) after the [only known] photograph by E. M. Sammis (1864). University of Washington Libraries, Special Collections, NA1515.

Meanwhile, an 1865 ordinance passed by the newly incorporated town of Seattle banned permanent Indian homes within city limits, forcing the chief to consider leaving the place named after him. Chief Seattle died at the Suquamish Reservation (Port Madison), Washington.

Urban Settlements

Major urban settlements in the Pacific Northwest were established or incorporated in the mid-19th century. These are Victoria and Vancouver (British Columbia), Seattle and Vancouver (Washington), and Portland (Oregon). The only city of the above that no other urban settlement in the area, or anywhere else in the world, bears its name is Seattle. What all these cities have in common is their location on a breathtaking coastal landscape (Fig. 6). The brief sketches below give a few details about each of these cities in the first decades after they emerged.

Figure 6. Coastal landscape in the Pacific Northwest. Photo by the author, 2013.

The site of the modern-day city of *Victoria* was known to the Coast Salish people as Camosun. One of the oldest cities in the Pacific Northwest, in which British settlement began in the early 1840s, Victoria soon became the most important city in Western Canada, becoming the capital of the united colonies of Vancouver Island and British Columbia in 1866. The population of the city at that time was only 3,630 [15]. The arrival of the Canadian Pacific Railway at Burrard Inlet, near Vancouver, BC in 1886 made that city an international port, connected to the rest of North America by rail. As a result, commercial activity in Victoria declined substantially, although the city and region continued to grow.

The city of *Vancouver, BC* was incorporated in 1886 (the same year that the first transcontinental train arrived). Canadian Pacific Railway President W. Van Horn arrived in Port Moody to establish a railroad station and gave the city its name in honor of G. Vancouver. The Great Vancouver Fire in the summer of 1886 destroyed the entire city. Following this event, the Vancouver Fire Department was established and the city was quickly rebuilt. Vancouver's population grew rapidly from a settlement of 1,000 people in 1881 to over 20,000 by the turn of the century and 100,000 by 1911 [12, p. 780].

The first European visit to what is now *Seattle* was in 1792 when Captain Vancouver made his expedition for the British Royal Navy to chart the Pacific Northwest. European settlement in the area began about six decades later, as early as 1851, when Arthur Denny and his group, known as the Denny Party, arrived here from Portland (OR) in the schooner *Exact* [19]. By the time the first European settlers arrived, the people later called the Duwamish tribe occupied at least 17 villages in the Elliot Bay area. The settlement on the east coast of Elliott Bay was founded in 1852 and, as mentioned above, was named Seattle in honor of the white-friendly chief of two local tribes. A recognizable landmark of modern-day Seattle is the Space Needle—an observation tower built in 1961 (Fig. 7).

The American city of *Vancouver, WA* is located in the very south of Washington State, on the north bank of the Columbia River, directly opposite Portland, located on the south bank of this river, from where Oregon begins to the south. Together, these cities form the Portland-Vancouver metropolitan area. The city was originally founded in 1825 around Fort Vancouver, a fur trading outpost. City officials have periodically proposed changing the name of the U.S. city back to Fort Vancouver to reduce confusion with its larger, more known neighbor to the north, Vancouver, BC.

Portland, an Oregon settlement named after Portland, Maine, began to be settled in the 1830s. Access to water provided convenient transportation of goods, and the lumber industry was a major force in the city's early business and economy. At the turn of the 20th century, the city had a strong reputation as one of the most dangerous port cities in the world, a center for organized crime and racketeering. After the city's economy experienced industrial growth during World War II, its negative reputation began to decline. Beginning in the 1960s, Portland became known for its growing progressive political values, earning it a new reputation as a counterculture stronghold [20].

Figure 7. The Space Needle in Seattle. Photo by the author, 2014.

Territorial Units

Despite the similar circumstances of their emergence, as well as close cultural and demographic factors, the territorial units that make up the Pacific Northwest belonged to different countries from the first decades of their foundation and, as such, went through a somewhat different history. Let us trace the main stages of this history, beginning with the formation of each separate territorial unit and the story of its name.

British Columbia

The province's name was chosen by Queen Victoria, when the mainland in front of the Vancouver Island, became a British colony in 1858 [21]. The etymology of the name British Columbia, however, has several layers. Thus, Columbia in the name British Columbia refers to the Columbia District, the British name for the territory drained by the Columbia River, which flows from the Canadian Rockies into the American state of Washington. The river, in turn, took its name from the Columbia Rediviva, an American ship that was extensively used in the Pacific Northwest maritime fur trade, while Columbia in the name of the ship came from a reference to Christopher Columbus. British in the name British Columbia was chosen by the queen to distinguish the British section of the district from that, which belonged to the United States and became the Oregon Territory a decade earlier [22].

Although today British Columbia is considered one of the most beautiful and lively places to live in North America, research shows that family letters between British Columbia and England between 1858 and 1914 describe the province as quiet and somewhat dull [23], while the population of the province quickly doubled in a decade (1871–1881, a few years before the Pacific Railroad arrived at Burrard Bay), reaching 17,000 white settlers out of a total population of approximately 53,000, half of whom were indigenous [23, p. 17].

Washington

There is only one state in the United States named after an American president, and that is Washington State.

Washington, or officially the state of Washington was formed from the western part of the Washington Territory, which was transferred to the British Empire in 1846 in accordance with the Oregon Treaty (border agreement). Bordered by the Pacific Ocean to the west, Oregon to the south, Idaho to the east, and the Canadian province of British Columbia to the north, the state was admitted to the United States as the 42nd state in 1889. Olympia is the capital of the state; the largest city is Seattle.

Washington State was so named by an act of the United States Congress during the creation of Washington Territory in 1853; the territory was to be named *Columbia* after the Columbia River and the Columbia District, but according to historical records, Kentucky Representative Richard H. Stanton thought the name was too similar to the District of Columbia (which contains the city of Washington, the nation's capital), and proposed name the new territory after President Washington [24].

Confusion over the state of Washington and the city of Washington, D.C. led to proposals to rename the state, including an 1889 proposal to name *Tacoma*. All these proposals were not supported. Finally, to avoid confusion, Washington is often referred to as *Washington State* to distinguish it from the nation's capital, *Washington, D.C.* [25].

Oregon

Oregon is a U.S. state bordering Washington along the Columbia River (most of the northern border) and Idaho along the Snake River (most of the eastern border). The 42nd parallel north defines the southern border with California and Nevada.

The name *Oregon* is of Spanish origin. The term *orejón* (meaning "big ear") comes from the historical chronicle *Relación de la Alta y Baja California* [Relationship of Upper and Lower California] written in 1598 by Rodrigo Montezuma of New Spain; it mentioned the Columbia River when Spanish explorers entered North America, which became part of the Viceroyalty of New Spain. This chronicle is the first topographical and linguistic source regarding the toponym Oregon.

Before the first European traders and settlers began exploring what is now Oregon's Pacific coast in the early mid-16th century, the land was inhabited for many centuries by two bands of indigenous *Chinook* people—the *Multnomah* and the *Clackamas* [26]. American settlers began arriving there in the 1800s. The first autonomous government was formed in the Oregon Country in 1843, and the Oregon Territory was created five years later. Oregon became the 33rd state of the U.S. in 1859.

Salem, a city located in the center of the Willamette Valley, is the capital of Oregon. It was founded in 1842, became the capital of the Oregon Territory nine years later, and was incorporated in 1857. As of 2019, 175 thousand people lived in the city.

Regional Administration and Disputes

From the early 16th century, formal claims to ownership of what is now British Columbia, Washington, and Oregon were maintained by Spain on the basis of the overland voyage of Núñez de Balboa, a Spanish explorer who happened to be the first European to reach the West Coast from the Americas. During the next two centuries, Russian fur traders came to the region from the north, that is, from Alaska—the then Russian Pacific coast of North America—to maintain their claims, mainly through the activity of Russian-America companies. Along with attempts to the extension of Spanish claims toward the north, Captain Cook's and Captain Vancouver's expeditions advanced British claims.

The United States has claimed the same region since the early 19th century based on the voyage of Robert Gray (1792) and the Lewis and Clark Expedition (1804), as well as the establishment of Fort Astoria in 1811. According to the 1818 Convention, the watershed was established on the territory delineating the border between British North America and the United States, on the condition that the western part be jointly administered by the two countries. At the same time, the U.S. government called this region the Oregon Country, and the British government called it British Columbia.

Although during the American Civil War (1861–1865) the local government of British Columbia tried to push London to invade and take control of the Washington Territory, the British government did not dare to go to war with the United States [27, pp. 19–20].

Population and Culture

The administrative divisions of the Pacific Northwest that belonged to the British Crown, the U.S. government, or both by being jointly administered until the 1850s share many common cultural traits while retaining their characteristics in each of them. The waves and composition of settlement and immigration in the area depended on the rules set by each territory, leading to a different demographic makeup in the region's cities over the decades. Thus, immigrants from Hong Kong and India began to settle in the cities of British Columbia in the decades following World War II, taking advantage of the opportunities provided by the British Crown to citizens of former colonies who wish to remain British subjects and live in the country of the British Commonwealth. In contrast, the new settlers of the U.S. Pacific Northwest were either immigrants from both Asia and other countries, or settlers who came there from other U.S. states, including African Americans, whites, and Hispanics. They usually arrived by land.

So, what is specific (and also common) in the culture of different places in the Pacific Northwest?

Language, Religion, and Politics

Pacific Northwest English is considered (by both Americans and Canadians) to be indistinguishable from speech in the U.S. Midwest. However, it is affected by the "Canadian raising," especially in British Columbia and, to a lesser extent, in Washington. Some point to the "California vowel shift" which can also be heard in regional speech.

While many consider Anglo-American, Anglo-Canadian, and Scandinavian-American culture to be the dominant culture in the Pacific Northwest, influences from Chinese, Mexican, and Native American cultures are among the characteristics of the region's cultural palette. Half the population of Vancouver, British Columbia reports English as a second language, whereas parts of Oregon and Washington are rather bilingual (English and Spanish).

Over the recent decades, the region as a whole is characterized by a multicultural environment, counterculture (especially in Portland, OR), and LGBT support (mainly in Vancouver, BC but also in Seattle), which received various manifestations, including in the church life at different levels as will be discussed later in the book.

According to recent studies and statistics, Pacific Northwesters reported the lowest levels of church attendance and religious affiliation among Canadian and U.S. citizens and residents, at about 25% in Washington and Oregon (as of 2008) and 44% in British Columbia (as of 2011) [28, 29].

There is a political divide between the more populated urban areas west of the mountains, which traditionally support left-wing parties on U.S. and Canadian political maps, and the less populated rural areas east of the mountains and in northern British Columbia, where people are more religious and support right-wing parties. In general, the Pacific Northwest has traditionally been the most liberal part of North American society.

Educational and Cultural Institutions

The Pacific Northwest is rich in public and private universities and colleges, some of which are highly ranked nationally, regionally, and globally. Thus, as of 2021, the University of British Columbia (UBC), located in Vancouver and Okanagan, BC ranks second in Canada and 34th in the world (or 13th based on its overall contributions to research and stewardship). The University of Washington located in Seattle ranks fifth among public universities in the United States and 25th in the world. There are many other public, private, or community colleges that provide affordable learning environments and offer their own areas of study, such as indigenous studies, forestry, urban studies, or Christian education.

Museums throughout the Pacific Northwest are characterized by their focus on coastal art, lifestyle, and indigenous history, such as the Royal British Columbia Museum, located in Victoria, BC, with its photo and audio-video collections; the Suquamish Museum (Suquamish, WA), which houses evidence of the Suquamish and Duwamish tribes and Chief Seattle; the Anthropological Museum on the UBC Campus in Vancouver; and some other institutions.

Many art galleries in any of the major cities in the Pacific Northwest offer traditional and contemporary coastal art created by artists from Alaska to Oregon. Some galleries focus on techniques or themes that are typical of local art. Thus, perhaps the richest collection of contemporary art with a deeply traditional background is offered by Quintana Galleries in Portland, Oregon. The original engravings by local artists presented here are of a very high level of concept and performance.

Walking through the galleries, museums, and even the streets of the cities of the Pacific Northwest is a true coastal life experience that you will not find anywhere else (Fig. 8).

Figure 8. Totem poles on display at the Anthropological Museum of the University of British Columbia in Vancouver. Photo by the author, 2014.

Chapter 2

Christianity in British Columbia, Washington, and Oregon

European settlement in the Pacific Northwest began as a trading, or at any rate commercial, enterprise. As was customary in any place where European and British colonists settled, many institutions associated with the Western way of life sprang up, most notably schools, hospitals, and churches. The latter as administrative institutions, physical objects, and spiritual stewardship in historical retrospect and the present are the subject of this chapter, which traces Christian institutions, communities, and practices in the Canadian and American Pacific Northwest.

A recent study examining religion and regionalism in American public life revealed the idiosyncrasies of the Pacific Northwest. "The distinctiveness had everything to do with the region's low degree of religious identification—something that had been the case ever since Anglo-Americans began settling the place in the 19th century," Silk notes.

In a place where institutional religion for non-indigenous peoples had never been strong, success required a high degree of enterprise on the one hand and, on the other, a pulling together on the part of religious communities that, elsewhere in the country, had historically kept their distance [30].

Land, Faith, and Voice: Christian Music in the Pacific Northwest
Alexander Rosenblatt
Copyright © 2024 Jenny Stanford Publishing Pte. Ltd.
ISBN 978-981-5129-11-3 (Hardcover), 978-1-003-47332-9 (eBook)
www.jennystanford.com

We will start by defining "American religions" in the U.S. and Canada in general and the main divisions within white and missionary churches, then move on to the current agenda, philosophy, and approaches of the churches in the Pacific Northwest to various issues, concluding this part of the discussion with arguments and examples of the use of historical forms of worship by local Christian institutions, as well as rituals that have no direct (and even indirect) relationship to Christianity.

The "American Religions"

The circumstances of religious institutionalization in the United States developed in such a way that from the beginning of Western settlement until World War II, various Protestant churches and denominations dominated the white community. All American presidents (up to John F. Kennedy) have been Protestants. The war changed the vision of things. In 1948, the World Council of Churches was founded by the ecumenical movement, followed two years later by the reorganization of the National Council of Churches (instead of the Federal Council) in the United States. The Holocaust in Europe pushed American Jews to the decision that such a tragedy should never happen again, which led, on the one hand, to support the establishment of the State of Israel, and, on the other hand, to the consolidation of the Abrahamic religions in America.

In practice,

> the trinity of the Protestant, Catholic, and Jewish faiths came increasingly to be recognized as the "American religions" ... [or] "religion of the American way of life," which meant that to call oneself a Protestant, a Catholic, or a Jew was simply a way of saying that one was an American [31].

In 1955, the trinity was somewhat canonized by sociologist Will Herberg in *Protestant–Catholic–Jew*, a study of American religious history. This union of American religions lasted as a mainstream until the mid-1990s, when the religious and demographic composition of U.S. citizens changed and new religious movements and political interests emerged.

The situation in Canada appears to be fairly similar in this regard: although "Canadian religions" are not articulated in the way it was in America, interreligious unions among white Canadians have shown exactly the same trend in recent decades—most such unions are either between descendants of Protestant and Catholic families or between any of them and persons of Jewish origin.

White Churches

Many residents of Seattle, Oregon, and Greater Vancouver continue to attend the churches their parents attended, but in recent decades, people have become very sensitive to the current agenda of one church or another.

Historically, churches on the North American continent reflect a retrospective of denominations specific to the English and other northern European worlds, current at the time of the arrival of the settlers. Along with the Catholics, many Protestants founded churches in a familiar environment.

Some of these churches emphasized ritual details (as did the Baptists and Methodists), while others focused on the practices and details of sanctuaries, miracles, and other metaphysical things (such as Presbyterians, Disciples of Christ, and any divisions associated with evangelicalism). Some of them were dedicated to delving into the Jewish roots of Christianity (Seventh-day Adventists, for example). In addition, new denominations emerged, such as the Latter-Day Saints (better known as Mormons), perhaps the only church in Christendom to officially practice (until 1890) plural marriage [33].

By the end of the 20th century, most of these churches began to be distinguished not by the initial emphasis of each of them on one or another aspect of ritual or scripture, but by the acceptability (or unacceptability) of the liberal values of modern society and—still—the attitude toward the authority of the Bible. The two groups of churches—the mainline and the evangelical—represent a modern divide within American and Canadian Christianity in the face of an ever-decreasing number of Christian believers (this point will be discussed separately).

Mainline Churches

"Mainline Protestant" is a fairly recent term to group white historic Protestant denominations in the United States associated with religious liberalism. This group, sometimes named *Seven Sisters of American Protestantism*, includes the following local Christian bodies: Baptist Churches, Disciples of Christ, Episcopal Church, Lutheran Church (in America), Presbyterian Church, United Church, and Methodist Church [34]. According to various studies in the last decade or so, other smaller denominations can also be considered part of the Mainline Protestant body.

Until recently, despite the name "mainline," the churches of this group were inferior in terms of the number of parishioners to institutional "competitors," that is, Evangelicals and Catholics. However, a 2020 study found that the number of parishioners in this group outnumbered Evangelicals for the first time in decades [35].

Evangelical Churches

One has to distinguish between "evangelicalism" as a worldwide interdenominational movement within Protestantism and "Evangelicalism" (with a capital 'E'), which is a uniquely American phenomenon that arose at the intersection of homegrown trends and influences of the 19th century, such as premillennialism and revivalism, and the synergy of religious practice with the political agenda and "America first" patriotism.

While Evangelicals, who until 2014 made up a quarter of the total number of Christians in the U.S. [36], recognize the Bible as the objective, authoritative word of God, for Mainline Protestants, the Bible becomes the word of God upon encounter (or rather existential encounter) with it. With this perception of the Bible as a human book that includes the words of God, the mainline stance leaves room for myths or errors in such cornerstone things as creation, virgin birth, resurrection, and the like.

Some parishes, usually associated with Mainline Protestantism, adhere to more evangelical views. Such are the separate wings of the Episcopal Churches in the United States and the Anglican Churches in Canada. Most white Evangelicals are associated with the right wing of the American political map, while Mainline Protestants traditionally vote for the left-wing parties. Black Protestants are not usually classified as either evangelical or mainline, and being more evangelical (with a small 'e') and religiously conservative, they vote for parties associated with social justice.

Dynamics of Attendance

Today (2023), a year after the two-year social paralysis caused by the COVID-19 pandemic, it is too early to sum up the decline in church attendance in the U.S. and Canada (if so), but some trends can already be identified.

Studies conducted over the past decade [35, 36] point to different trends and figures regarding the balance between Mainline and Evangelical churches and the very tendency for the growth or decline of Christian organizations in general and these groups in particular. However, since the primary purpose of this book (and this chapter) is to provide sufficient information about church life and practice in the Canadian and American parts of the Pacific Northwest, the focus will be on data for that particular region.

The Canadian research carried out in 2016 says that "Mainline Protestant churches that focus on the gospel and prayer are growing, while those that don't are in decline" [37]. The questionnaire included sentences for clergy's and congregation's agreement/disagreement that touched both "evangelical" and "mainline" principal points, such as: "The beliefs of the Christian faith need to change over time to stay relevant" or "Jesus rose from the dead with a real flesh and blood body, leaving behind an empty tomb." The 2022 study [30] says that life no longer revolves around church and some of the Canadian churches (Anglican church, for example) will die out by 2040...

Some of the recent studies [e.g., 35] are rather optimistic that the mainline churches have set a moderate line acceptable to their parishioners (who, according to the experience of the author of this book, were really shocked in 2013–2014 by the revolutionary change in the attitude of the church toward traditional Christian values) and are on the rise. The 2019 study of religiosity (more precisely, non-religiousness) of the Canadian and American Pacific Northwest [30] highlights environmentalism as the leading spiritual movement in this region, which is rather non-religious in terms of traditional religiosity. The study also notes that evangelical churches in British

Columbia, Washington, and Oregon have become more sensitive to liberal and environmental trends.

Missionary Churches

The Pacific Northwest is rich in various indigenous churches. The missionary work among local residents was on the agenda for both Catholic and Protestant priests and missionaries from the very beginning of the white settlement and up to the mid-1990s. Thus, the system of residential schools in Canada was aimed at the complete assimilation of indigenous people. The Christian faith was part of this agenda. Under a Canadian government program running from the late 1800s to 1996, First Nations, Métis, and Inuit children were removed from their families and placed in residential schools. The first residential school to open in British Columbia was St. Mary's Residential School in Mission opened in 1867. It was also the last one in the province, closed in 1984 [39]. The aim of the American missionaries acting without any special program was also to assimilate the natives, making them "English in their language, civilized in their habits, and Christian in their religion" [40].

Although missionary activity has been only partially successful, various churches have sprung up throughout the region. The congregation of these churches comes from indigenous communities, while the spiritual leaders are white or local. Some of these churches belong to major denominations in whose name the missionaries acted. The other part is the churches that follow their own unique theology and ritual. Such, for example, is the *Indian Shaker Church*, a Christian denomination founded in 1881 by the Squaxin shaman John Slocum and his wife Mary Slocum in Washington state [41, p. 3]. Most Indian Shakers accept direct contact with God without the need for a Bible. Their worship lasts hours and includes the elements of Catholic and Protestant service enriched with shamanic practices, accompanied by a very loud sound of handbells. This church, which is said to have ten to twenty active congregations in British Columbia, Washington, and Oregon, is not affiliated with the historical Shaker congregations that developed from Anne Lee's doctrine on celibacy and that existed between 1776 and the early 21st century, whereupon Shakers gradually dwindled to one active congregation that has less than ten members [42].

Figure 9. Blessed Kateri Tekekwitha, as reproduced in Seeing a New Day: A 150 Year History of St. Peter Catholic Mission. Suquamish, WA: Port Madison Indian Reservation, 2012, p. 23.

Indigenous congregations, along with the saints shared by Christians around the world, have their own saints, such as Blessed Kateri Tekekwitha (Fig. 9), who "devoted her short life (1656–1680) to teaching prayers to children, and helping the sick and the aged" [43, p. 23].

Symbols of Faith

The symbols most commonly associated with Christianity are the Cross (with or without the crucified) and the image of the Mother and Child. However, there are some other, more indirect symbols that are also associated with this religion. Along with the snake, which for many represents a sign of temptation, the fish symbol (Fig. 10a) is a secret sign used by early Christians: The word *Ichthus* ("fish" in Greek) is used as an abbreviation for Jesus Christ, Son of God, and Savior [44, p. 176]. Another such symbol is an image of three nails (Fig. 10b). Used during crucifixion to attach hands and feet to the cross, three nails symbolize the supreme sacrifice of Jesus Christ [44, p. 177].

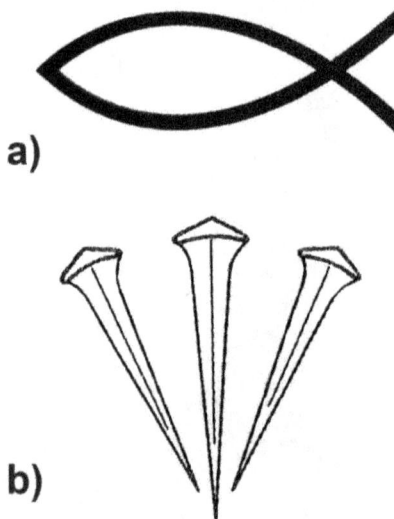

a)

b)

Figure 10. Indirect christian symbols, as reproduced in m. Bruce-Mitford, *Signs & Symbols: an Illustrated Guide to Their Origins and Meanings*. London: Dorling Kindersley, 2019, pp. 176–177.

As the most non-religious region in both the U.S. and Canada, with many local churches, the Pacific Northwest exemplifies the use of traditional and modern modified symbols for its Christian institutions. Perhaps most convincing in design and meaning is the logo of Christ Church Cathedral in Victoria, British Columbia (Fig. 11). This image in the most symbolic way, avoiding direct associations, simultaneously reminds of three nails, a snake, a cross, and the crucified.

Figure 11. Logo of the Christ Church Cathedral, Victoria, BC.

Statistical Data

This section will present statistical data on the confessional map in its dynamics, on various collections of hymns and other liturgical/ service books, as well as on church buildings, accompanied by a number of relevant images and figures.

Denominations

Two studies independently conducted by Washington, DC-based institutions—the Pew Research Center (data collected in 2007 and 2014) [36] and the Public Religion Research Institute (2020 Census of American Religion) [35]—show completely different figures regarding the distribution of Americans between churches.

While the percentage of Christians in the United States (in general) has not changed at about 70 percent, in the states of Washington and Oregon this number is about 60 percent (even less in British Columbia), and the number of non-believers in the same places is higher by 10–20% compared to the average for these countries, the indication of "mainline" and "evangelical" groups of Protestants deserves attention. While the 2014 study contains data both on the grouping of churches according to their views and the percentage for each denomination within those groups, the 2020 study only looks at the distribution among Protestant congregations according to the general definitions above and color factor. Both groups in the 2014 study include the same denominations in each of them, marked "evangelical tradition" or "mainline tradition" for each. This points to a recent split in Protestant denominations (beginning around 2005). The 2020 census does not provide data for individual churches within the general groupings, as differences between denominations already seem small amid differences in the agenda. The 2020 study also excludes black and color Protestants from the evangelical/mainline split, although figures for the latter churches (which are evangelical in their theology) could result in a similar total to the 2014 study.

Hymnals and Service Books

The large number of Protestant churches in the United States and Canada (multiplied by the evangelical/mainline divide) cannot but be reflected in the abundance and variety of hymnbooks published or in one way or another associated with them.

Throughout the 1990s, most Protestant denominations produced new editions of hymnbooks, some of which were shared by several churches. When the schism between evangelical and mainline churches divided nearly all white Protestant churches, the question arose of which hymnbooks to use in churches associated with either the "evangelical tradition" or the "mainline tradition." Whenever an official branch of a Protestant church maintained the mainline ideology and produced new, politically correct hymnbooks in which depiction of God as *Father* and *Lord* gave way to definitions such as *All-inclusive One* or *Great Spirit*, the clergy of the evangelical wing of the respective churches preferred using either the old hymnbooks associated with their church, or new hymnal books produced by the evangelical wings of other Protestant churches, or instead hymnals issued elsewhere, such as Kenya or Rwanda, where the hymns followed a clear evangelical content, including traditional wording.

Unlike Protestant churches, successive editions of *Worship* (first issued in 1971) used in the Catholic Churches in the United States and Canada can be treated as a single source. However, the reality of the Pacific Northwest shows that *Worship II* (1975 edition) is still the title of choice. This edition, as explained in the editor's preface, reflects "American 'melting pot' culture" [45, Preface], which supports the use of hymns as a genre commonly associated with Protestant culture in Roman Catholic churches. One of the main differences between *Worship* and *Worship II* is the reverse use of "thee" and "thy" instead of the modern "you" and "your" in the hymn lyrics. St. James Cathedral in Seattle, for example, still uses this edition, which can be found as pew books in the church, although two newer editions have since come out.

Church Buildings

Variety of churches in British Columbia, Washington, and Oregon—whether historical or modern; white, missionary, or autochthonous—suggests that an appropriate variety of styles and architectural solutions will be found in the exterior and interior of the buildings in which these churches are located. Indeed, many of the white churches—whether cathedrals or parish churches—are recognizable both inside and out, such as the interior of St. James Catholic Cathedral in Seattle (Fig. 12).

Figure 12. St. James Cathedral in Seattle. Photo by the author, 2021.

Missionary churches built over the years throughout the Pacific Northwest were intended to accommodate small to medium-sized local congregations. Most of these churches, like white Protestant and Catholic parish churches, followed regional patterns of timber-frame construction using clapboard (wood or, later, drywall) or, in some cases, stone buildings. A unique collection of photographs of indigenous churches in British Columbia, provided with essential information about the history and current state of these churches and their parishes [4], gives an idea of both the scope of missionary work and the result of the creation of Christian communities. Some of these churches are quite unique in their appearance or some of the accessories in the courtyard. Such is the bell tower near St. Paul's church in Kitwanga, BC covered with clapboard in the early 2000s (Fig. 13).

Figure 13. Bell tower near St. Paul's Church in Kitwanga, BC. Photo by K. E. Perry, 2007, as reproduced in *Heritage Churches of the Indigenous Peoples of British Columbia,* Surrey, BC: Hancock House, 2019, p. 218.

Autochthonous churches associated with congregations that came to Christianity with their own vision of worship and related practices represent another group of churches with their own patterns of architectural solutions. The buildings of such churches are rather wide than high, since they are intended for parishes larger than the parishes of missionary churches. As is customary in white and missionary churches, autochthonous church buildings may combine a higher section (usually a bell tower) and a wider section (prayer hall), as at Indian Shaker Church in Marysville, WA (Fig. 14).

Figure 14. Indian Shaker Church in Marysville, WA. Photo by the author, 2021.

Current Agenda

The very concept of "current agenda" in relation to Christianity in the United States and Canada, and more specifically in the Pacific Northwest, is a concept to be applied to about 30 percent of all Christian believers, namely white Protestants. For other Christians, the agenda is actually more internal or even historical, but not necessarily "current." However, some modern trends have made their way into non-white communities, while other idiosyncrasies, references, and forms of worship have also influenced Catholic and non-white Protestant services.

The current agenda of Mainline Protestants goes hand in hand with the agenda of modern liberal society, including support for the weaker social strata and, especially, LGBT communities, who are not so much looking for such support themselves, but the church supports them at the suggestion of organizations that initially support them. As a result, mainline churches welcome same-sex marriages performed in accordance with the church rite. Another trend in the mainline current agenda is the acknowledgment of sin as part of the human condition. In contrast to the advanced views of the mainline clergy, they are dressed in a very traditional way. The music of the service is also quite traditional.

The evangelical division recognizes modern liberal currents but does not consider them the official policy of the church as a traditionally conservative element of society and its management. Following this agenda, the evangelical clergy broke away from the correspondent mainline denominations and focused on traditional Christian values and practices. Yet, they support the appearance of clergymen in non-traditional clothes. The music in their churches includes praise songs in the "church rock" style associated with the 1980s. Thus, both sides of the split have something of an advanced vision, while the other parts are on quite traditional paths.

The former missionary churches of the indigenous communities have their own views on the current agenda, corresponding to their social needs. One of the local churches in Marysville, WA, for example, displayed an LGBT flag on the facade of the church building, and the slogans "Black Lives Matter" and "Native Lives Matter" on the windows (Fig. 15).

Other aspects of church innovations have much less to do with politics or splits in white Protestant churches. Local (native) customs, various borrowings from the visions and experiences of the Far East, as well as the restoration of a historical type of worship or inventions/events aimed at conciliatory activity are also part of the current agenda.

Figure 15. Local church building in Marysville, WA (fragment). Photo by the author, 2021.

Native Customs and Practices

While only a few indigenous congregations (or congregations of which native people are a part) can be counted within the Mainline and Evangelical Protestant churches as well as Catholic churches in the Pacific Northwest, the very presence of native peoples and their customs and practices is enriching and, to a certain extent, create an atmosphere of worship.

Figure 16.   The priest shows a mantle with an embroidered cross and a badge of prestige, presented to him. Photo by the author, 2013.

For example, during a service at the Christ Church Anglican cathedral in Vancouver, BC, a priest invites the congregation to stand up and turn to the east (and then to other directions), explaining the significance of such gestures in the historical beliefs of the indigenous peoples. The traditional *healing circle* is held weekly at a small church in New Westminster, BC, which is attended mostly by a few older people from the major, Hispanic, part of this parish.

If unmixed native Christian communities maintain their own unique rituals (as the Indian Shakers do), then missionary and even more post-missionary churches in the Pacific Northwest show a fair amount of sensitivity both to the specific customs of native Christianity and to the original, i.e., pre-Christian culture in their services. For example, at Christ Church Cathedral in Victoria, BC, there was a weekly litany of reconciliation prior to the COVID pandemic, during which the ringing of a single bell was used as a reminder of the custom of Indian Shakers, themselves a hallmark of indigenous Christianity.

A unique in its kind example of the mutual respect was presented in a small Anglican parish in Vancouver, BC: Native parishioners presented the priest with a mantle with an embroidered cross and a badge of prestige from the Nisga'a people shortly after the priest learned the Nisga'a language in order to recite the key words of the service specifically for the four families who attended this small church (Fig. 16).

Special Forms of Worship

Today, churches in the Pacific Northwest practice more than just traditional forms of Christian service (that is, the Sunday Eucharist, morning and evening prayers). Special forms of these services are welcome, as well as other forms of worship or any other events initiated by the church.

In the first group of such events, the Celtic Eucharist is probably the most historical and authentic: it was practiced, at least until the COVID pandemic, at Christ Church Cathedral in Victoria, BC. Evening prayers with a pre-announced musical program performed by professional choirs are included in the weekly plan of any cathedral or large church.

There are other forms of public church services and gatherings. Among these, it is worth mentioning the Taizé worship, which originated in France in 1940 as an ecumenical monastic order with a strong commitment to peace and justice and characterized by "prayer and silence," which is a kind of Christian meditation. Taizé worship events are regularly held throughout the Pacific Northwest—in Victoria and Vancouver, BC; Seattle and Olympia, WA; Portland, OR; as well as in other cities of the region.

Meditation as a form of Christian prayer is supported by forms of church attendance such as hour-long silent prayer without public service in some cathedrals. Furthermore, Trinity Episcopal Cathedral in Portland, OR, offers a walk through the Labyrinth that has become something of a local hallmark. During our visit to the hall that houses the Labyrinth (and the art exhibition), the homeless were offered food. "There is no wrong way to walk the labyrinth. All are welcome!" the website of the cathedral says. This truly symbolic sentence is quite in line with the current agenda of the Episcopal Church, namely, its mainline division.

The interiors of many churches are of architectural interest. A relatively recent trend of churches housed in such buildings is architecture-music tours, such as a series of such events at Christ Church Cathedral in Victoria, BC, one of which is called *Harps and Angels*, which introduces the public to unique stained-glass windows of the church, an excursion ending with a harp concert. Flower arranging courses and art exhibitions are also part of the community outreach characteristic of the regional Christian institutions.

Chapter 3

Native Christian Art: Philosophy and Examples

This chapter reveals the philosophy and visual manifestations of indigenous peoples in relation to Christianity. The discussion will first focus on how respected indigenous leaders share their wisdom and worldview; what the church fathers think of the local peoples and their wisdom; and what local Christians say about themselves and their views on Christianity. However, the main part of the discussion consists of reflections on the visual concepts of Christian subjects in comparison with traditional and modern plots in the native art of the Pacific Northwest. A discussion of the appearance of local churches closes the circle of topics of the chapter.

The Wisdom of the Native People

The wisdom and philosophy of the indigenous inhabitants of the region did not go unnoticed by the first colonists. A clear indication of this was the collaboration between white merchants and Chief Seattle in the early 1850s. However, as far as we can judge today, the knowledge and valuable skills of the indigenous people of this area,

Land, Faith, and Voice: Christian Music in the Pacific Northwest
Alexander Rosenblatt
Copyright © 2024 Jenny Stanford Publishing Pte. Ltd.
ISBN 978-981-5129-11-3 (Hardcover), 978-1-003-47332-9 (eBook)
www.jennystanford.com

who lived here for thousands of years and perfectly knew how to preserve this land, remained largely neglected until the 1950s.

Gradually, ethnographers, anthropologists, and writers began to fill this gap in knowledge about the region and its residents. By the end of the millennium, a book was published entirely devoted to the wisdom and intelligence of the indigenous peoples of America [6]. To date, it is perhaps one of the most competent collections of thoughts expressed by the leaders of the indigenous tribes and communities of North America, as well as an attempt at an in-depth classification of the worldview of Native Americans. This book, along with other studies and publications on the subject, provides a detailed insight into the unique set of attitudes that exist among coastal and inland native people of the U.S. and Canada. The following is a summary of the worldview of the Pacific Northwest natives, as it seems to the author relevant for the purposes of the present book.

Land and Nature. Love for and unity with Land and Nature is one of the cornerstones in the life philosophy of indigenous people who prefer open spaces to palaces that will someday decay, while Nature will remain Nature. Another point regarding the land concerns the issue of ownership. Native wisdom tends to attribute the land to the Great Spirit rather than seeing it as the property of the natives or the whites.

Anti-Consumerism. From the point of view of Western sociology, the attitude of indigenous peoples toward issues of property and consumption can be defined as anti-consumerism, and not as minimalism, since the latter term corresponds to the lowest value in the range of minimum-optimum-maximum, and the former denies property and consumption as welfare institutions, referring to simplicity and "normal" needs for everything.

Integrity and Count. One of the fundamental differences in general concepts and customs between whites and locals is the perception of integrity and the method of counting in relation to naturally "indivisible" things. At the time of the meeting of cultures, the natives, for example, had difficulty accepting the Western method of dividing days into hours.

Word and Silence. While Western culture prioritizes the power of the Word, Native American wisdom attributes such power to Silence.

"Guard your tongue in youth, and in age you may mature a thought that will be of service to your people," the old chief said [6, 87]. When invited to dine with a local family, one can show respect to the host by silently smoking a pipe and walking away, rather than engaging in the "small talk" so common in Western dinners.

Justice. Indigenous peoples are endowed with a sense of justice. They could not come to terms with the practice of slavery that took place before their eyes in the first decades of the white settlement.

Although local leaders, most notably Seattle, chief of the Suquamish and Duwamish tribes, advocated cooperation with whites beginning in the 1830s, and such cooperation was successful throughout the 1850s, the desire of the colonists to resettle the natives on the reservations became apparent early in that decade. This understanding and wisdom in accepting the situation culminated in a speech by Chief Seattle in 1853, immediately following the speech of the new governor of the then-created Washington Territory. This speech, recorded by many in several different versions, was full of sadness and hopelessness about the fate of his people. It was also a recognition of the fact that the two cultures cannot coexist easily and that the settlers are numerous and stronger than the natives. However, it was a call to his people to come to terms with this situation and see the whites as their protectors from other tribes, because otherwise there would still be nothing to do. "We may be brothers after all. We'll see," Seattle said at the end of his speech. This phrase is quoted in all sources where this event is mentioned.

Christianity and Local Beliefs

Historically, West Coasters have believed in the Great Spirit and the spirit of the ancestors. They preferred to talk about people rather than about God, arguing that talking about God is more likely to lead to quarrels than to explain and improve the human vision of the world. When native teenagers were taught Christianity, some of them asked questions regarding, in particular, metaphorical biblical descriptions, such as the order of creation, finding many "practical" inconsistencies that cast doubt on this religion in their eyes. Indigenous beliefs, on the contrary, can rather be described as a state of mind than a dogma.

However, the decades-long meeting of native beliefs with the inner essence of Christianity brought the positions of the two belief systems closer together. While even modern native religion is more like a temple of nature, the power of silence and silent prayer has become part of the Christian religion.

Figure 17. Frederick Alexcee. Baptismal Font, 1886, wooden carving, paint. Museum of Anthropology at UBC, Vancouver, BC. Gallery of Northwest Masterworks. Object No. A1776 a-c. Photo by the author, 2022.

The path of interpenetration of the two belief systems was not easy. Operating in different ways, the American missionaries south of the Columbia River and their British counterparts north of it did their part. No matter what balance between civil and religious oppression was applied to the natives in the territories of British Columbia or Washington, they all worked to drive the natives out of their lands, on the one hand, and on the other hand, converting them to Christianity. The century-old experience of residential schools in Canada, which consisted of forcibly removing children from indigenous families and placing them in closed Christian schools, had a very sad resonance among indigenous people. A striking example of this practice is the exhibit at the University of British Columbia Museum of Anthropology in Vancouver (Fig. 17), which consists of a wooden statue of an angel, or rather a priest, and a shotgun next to it. The statue was taken from one of the local churches in British Columbia, as children were afraid of it. The gun clearly symbolizes that Christianity among the natives was spread by force. An episode of the Canadian television series *Anne with an E* (internationally premiered on Netflix in 2017) follows a local parents' attempt to free their daughter from a residential school at the turn of the 20th century. The parents were forced to step back under the threat of gunfire from the white men who were guarding the school from the children's parents. Be that as it may, two-thirds of native Canadians today identify as Christians, multiple sources claim.

Native Christians: Perception and Self-Perception

Currently, the recognition of the indigenous peoples of the Pacific Northwest occurs at the state, municipal, academic, and religious levels. When you correspond for years with the officials of any college or university in Washington, Oregon, or British Columbia, you cannot help but notice the new lines under each signature, saying in whose territories this or that college is located and to which tribe or nation the college is grateful for the cooperation and friendship. If you visit the University of British Columbia in Vancouver once every few years, you cannot help but notice new, sometimes difficult to read, names in the Salish languages, in addition to the already familiar ones: Main Mall, Lower Mall, etc. "First Nations people have unique gifts and knowledge. When these are valued and recognized, we will contribute to the completion of the Christian community as God designed it to be," reads the North America Indigenous Ministries homepage.

And what do indigenous peoples themselves say about Christianity and their place in this religious community? Here is what the native Anglicans of Canada write about themselves:

> *We proclaim and celebrate the gospel of Jesus Christ in worship and action. But through the Grace of Jesus Christ we also affirm our traditional spirituality and our place in God's Creation. We know that Christ has come to fulfill our own traditions too.*
>
> *We have had the residential schools, which tore us from home and suppressed our traditions, our languages, our relationship with the land and the Creator—our very identities.*
>
> *Yet there have been times, too, when the churches have been our best support in the Canadian society—against those who coveted our land, who would see the death of our language and culture* [46].

Beyond the Missionary Work

In addition to missionary activity, alternative forms of Christianity have sprung up in the area, most notably the Indian Shaker Church. This church is very special compared to any contemporary church in the Pacific Northwest and is also exclusive to the region.

The denomination was founded in the early 1880s by John and Mary Slocum after John was miraculously healed of illness twice in a row. When John fell ill for the first time and was about to die, according to legend, he went to heaven and came face to face with God. He was lucky to return to Earth with a message from God to his people, instructing them not to drink alcohol, not to smoke, and not to gamble. However, he was the first to forget this instruction. When a year later he fell ill again and his father called an Indian doctor, nothing seemed to help. Then Mary left the house, ran to the shore, and began to tremble. Returning, still trembling, she called the people, prompting them to sing and ring the bells. After this practice, John came back to life again (this time to follow God's message), Indian doctors were banned by the locals (as if they had tried to kill John), and a new form of the Christian religion began [47, p. 5]. Why actually Christian? It was more of a coincidence of the colonial authorities to eliminate the practice of Indian doctors as inconsistent with the Western understanding of health care and the desire of the Slocums to compete with these doctors. The colonists acquainted the indigenous peoples with spiritual images of God and Jesus, and the Slocums adopted this.

The Indian Shaker Churches, which spread from Vancouver Island across the continental Pacific Northwest south to Northern California, are still active today, following the practice established in the early years and using no written sources at all. The agenda is that the word of God comes without a book.

Another manifestation of non-missionary Christianity is the Appreciation of Beauty, embedded in the original worldview and beliefs of the indigenous peoples of America. The Christian churches of the region follow this concept widely, in particular by organizing flower arranging courses in churches. However, at its core, this position simply suggests that there should be no direct imitation of God's creation. That is why the language of native art, especially coastal art, is so symbolic and unique.

Native Art: Tradition and Modernity

What is the art of the indigenous peoples of the Pacific Northwest? What is traditional and what is modern?

Unlike Western art, in which any period is associated with either style or technique, or both, indigenous art is much more consistent in its statements and always recognizable. Yet, the encounter with Western art and the availability of new techniques led over the decades to the evolution and crystallization of coastal art as it is presented today.

The Pacific Northwest has its own symbols that characterize the local art and reflect the beliefs and worldview of the people who have inhabited this area for thousands of years. If the traditional indigenous art of the region is commonly associated with totems— unmistakable carved wooden poles, then today two-color lithographs and serigraphs can be considered an equally noticeable form of the indigenous art of the region (see Fig. 18). Such artworks can be found in the art galleries throughout the cities of the Pacific Northwest. The artists who work in this technique represent Kwakwaka'wakw, Skokomish, Coast Salish, Tsimshian, and some other cultures. The current generation of local artists focuses on symbols of figures from the natural environment—wolf, raven, and fish, sometimes combined into a human image, with which they identify. These artworks are still "traditional."

Figure 18. David Boxley. Passages, 2012, serigraph, 107/150. Art Collection of Zefat Academic College, Israel. Object No. PNW007.

Modern native art is characterized, in particular, by a combination of realistic-style landscapes with the symbols of animals. These symbols resemble traditional printmaking: they even can be reproduced using this technique (see Fig. 19).

Figure 19. Richard Shorty. Reflection, c. 1988, mixed technique. Indigenous Collection Richmond, BC, Canada. Stock No. POD1139. Digital printout for retail sale.

Another approach of a native artist to modern or, more precisely, modernist art is to take a typical Western image and make it "his own" [48, description for Plate 220]. Fig. 20 reproduces an example of such an approach to an art object.

Figure 20. Wooden model of a sewing machine decorated with totemic design (Tlingit tribe), as reproduced in R. B. Inverarity, *Art of the Northwest Coast Indians*, Berkely: University of California Press, 1950, Plate 220.

Christian Plots in the Native Art

Christian symbols appeared in the applied art of the indigenous craftsmen of the Northwest at the end of the 19th century, when the first indigenous Christian communities arose there. The Maltese cross and its other forms can be seen on various embroidery patterns and household items (Fig. 21). This feature of local craftsmanship has not gone unnoticed by other artists, notably renowned Pacific Northwest-born glass artist Dale Chihuly. Chihuly began his artistic career in weaving by taking weaving classes at the University of Washington, where he first incorporated glass shards into woven tapestries back in 1963. In the Northwest Room of the Chihuly Garden and Glass exhibition in Seattle, there is a glass vessel made in the style of native weaving, with a cross clearly visible in the "textile" pattern (Fig. 22).

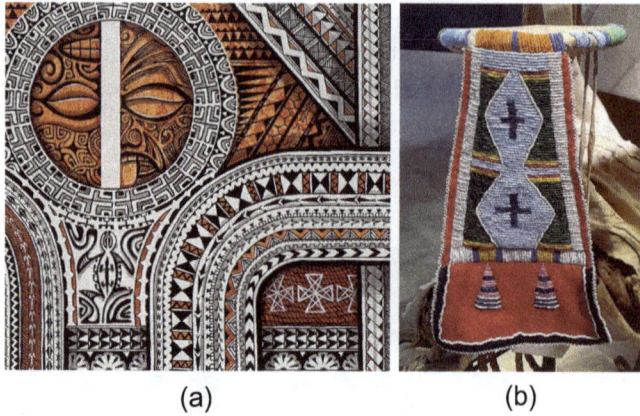

(a)   (b)

Figure 21. (a, b) Examples of the Pacific Northwest native craftmanship at the Burke Museum of Natural History and Culture, Seattle, Washington. Photos by the author, 2021.

Symbols aside, Christian subjects associated with both the Old and the New Bible receive a very peculiar treatment in native art. Actually, the artists are not burdened by the canon of Western painting, which obliges them to adhere to a certain tradition or style, they are independent in their views on Christianity, and the artistic results are therefore as unpredictable as they are impressive.

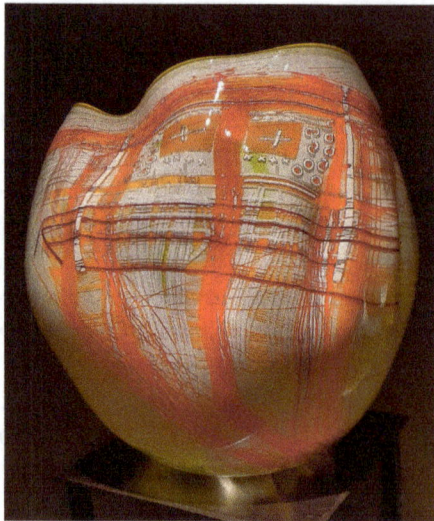

Figure 22. Dale Chihuly. *Glass vessel*. Chihuly Garden and Glass, Seattle, Washington, Northwest Room. Photo by the author, 2021.

The vivid example of an indigenous artist's vision of the Old (Hebrew) Bible, Genesis, the woman through whom the family tree continues to Jesus and the Cross, is presented in a 1968 watercolor *Tree of Jesse* by C. Terry Saul (Fig. 23).

Figure 23. C. Terry Saul. Tree of Jesse, 1968, watercolor on paper, as reproduced in M. Archuleta and R. Strickland. *Shared Visions. Native American Painters and Sculptors in the Twentieth Century*. New York: The New Press, 1991, p. 46.

Some other ideas and visions, which might rather diverge from Christian themes, were surprisingly implemented in response to the Canadian Conference of Catholic Bishops' call for national artists to share their vision of Christianity in 1975. Many artists across the country, including indigenous artists who consulted with their elders and used their own sacred symbols to convey the Christian message, submitted their works, some of which were posted on the "Indigenous Art Collection," the online resource of the *Canadian Conference of Catholic Bishops* [49].

Figure 24. Jackson Beardy. Nativity, c. 1975, acrylic on canvas, posted on the online resource "Indigenous Art Collection" of the *Canadian Conference of Catholic Bishops* [49, "Nativity"].

One of these works, *Nativity* by Jackson Beardy (Fig. 24), is accompanied by a detailed explanation of the artist about the images depicted, which is quoted below with small cuts:

It is my personal belief that a messenger from the Great Spirit came to earth in the form of His image after Him through a virgin birth in unrecorded history. Through this man, knowledge was passed onto man from the Great Spirit. Many of the teachings of this man have been kept by word of mouth through the ages by the elders of all tribes.

We see the virgin mother-to-be holding on to an embryo connected to the sun symbol (the Great Spirit) who has deemed it necessary to send his messenger to his people. The mother is also connected to Mother Earth who is nursing her. She too is connected by a lifeline to the sun symbol. Around her are all the orders of creatures who come to see the messenger. He is born to explain their existence, [to restore] harmony between humanity and the elements, physically, mentally, and spiritually. On the other side of the sun symbol we see an elder in prayer, ritually offering a bowl filled with sacred things. [...]

The four semicircles represent the elements of the air: snow, rain, tornadoes, heat. The moon is painted above the elder. We regard the moon as our Grandmother who keeps vigil over all creatures during the night [49, "Nativity"].

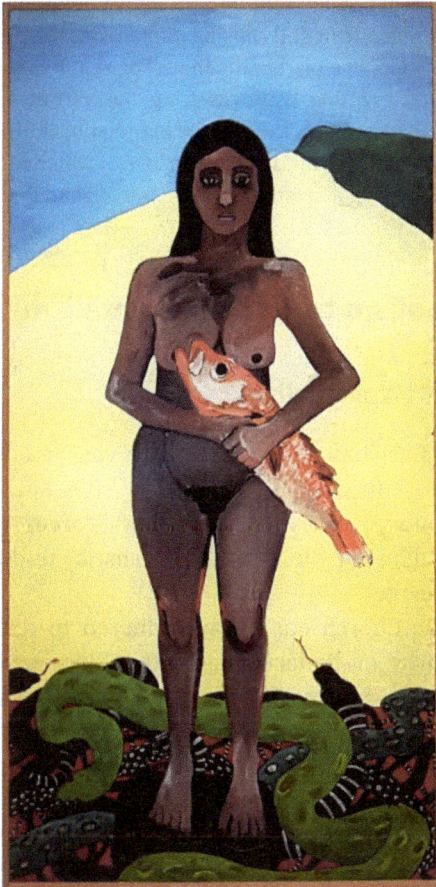

Figure 25. Joan Brown. *Eve with Fish and Snake*, 1970, oil on masonite. Seattle Art Museum. Photo by the author, 2018.

In the art museums of the Pacific Northwest, you can sometimes find artistic expression of these same combinations of local images with Christian plots and symbols in a rather unusual context or interpretation. Such is *Eve with Fish and Snake* (1970) from the "Paradise Series #1" by Joan Brown (Fig. 25). The work, which has been exhibited several times at the Seattle Museum of Art, is not currently on display at the museum as of summer 2022. However, it is listed on the museum's website, and the description for this work reads:

> In this painting of the biblical figure of Eve, Brown portrays her standing alone—without her male counterpart, Adam. Typically vilified for eating the forbidden fruit and causing humankind to be expelled from the Garden of Eden, Eve disregards the serpent at her feet that would lead her to the tempting fruit, resetting the narrative for the first woman. The fish in her hands is a recurring symbol in Brown's work; it may be a reference to the artist's lifelong love of water and competitive swimming, suggesting a kinship between herself and Eve [50].

From Symbolism to Environmentalism

Symbolism vs Hyperrealism

The images of Christian subjects that you can find throughout the Pacific Northwest in churches and other sites such as museums and various public places have varying degrees of symbolism, from images following the Western "realistic" tradition to highly sophisticated images.

The Catholic Church has always adhered to realistic imagery (albeit the works of Pieter Bruegel the Elder and Hieronymus Bosch seem rather "surreal" today). The Catholic churches of the Northwest are no exception. Some even host sculptural images of a hyper-realistic quality, such as the Catholic Proto-Cathedral of St. James the Greater in Vancouver, Washington. Most notable among the sculptures there is the group of the Holy Family at the entrance to the church on the left. St. Joseph is depicted here with a saw, which is a very realistic reminder to visitors of the occupation of Our Lady's husband (Fig. 26).

Figure 26. *The Holy Family*, unsigned, renovated by Conrad Schmitt Studios, Inc. in 2008. St. James Catholic Proto-Cathedral, Vancouver, Washington. Photo by the author, 2022.

Although realistic (and even hyper-realistic) ideas were not alien to indigenous Christian art of the late 19th century (such as the wood carving in Fig. 17 above), while early symbolism in European Christian art dates from around the same time (for example, the famous Yellow Christ, Green Christ, and Self-Portrait with the Yellow Christ by Paul Gauguin), in recent decades, the time has come for Christian native symbolic art. Examples of such art can be found in different places. Thus, the Legislative Assembly of the Washington State at Olympia held an exhibition in the summer of 2022 whose logo was taken from *The Prophet of Direction* (1989), a lithograph by Greg Colfax referred to as "silkscreen" in the Burke Museum database (Fig. 27).

Figure 27. Greg Colfax, *The Prophet of Direction*, 1989, silkscreen print, 52/150. Burke Museum of Natural History and Culture, Seattle, Washington, Contemporary Culture Collections, Object 1993-44/1.

Appearance of Indigenous Churches

While many of the cathedral churches in the cities of the Pacific Northwest are noted for their beauty and are well-equipped with organs, stained glass, woodwork, and sculpture, most indigenous church buildings are distinguished by a noble simplicity. The above book [4], entirely devoted to the appearance of the native churches of British Columbia, gives a true idea of the style of these churches. However, there is no mention of at least one church in this book, namely the Indian Shaker Church in Duncan, British Columbia.

It is not for nothing that no photograph of this church is not only in the book about indigenous heritage churches in British Columbia but also on the Internet. Only the locals tell how to find the way to it—Google Maps gives an erroneous address, and it is almost impossible to find the "hidden church" (Fig. 28) without a human prompt.

Figure 28. Duncan Indian Shaker Church, Duncan, British Columbia. Photo by the author, 2022.

In agreement with local residents, neither a photo of the interior of this church nor its detailed location is given here. The church is active, while the service is traditional for this denomination: it lasts two to three hours and is accompanied by singing and ringing of bells.

The simplicity of the building design is more indicative of the indigenous approach to how the house of worship should look like than of the lack of funds allocated for the maintenance and development of such a place. Meetings with the natives in other, ethnically diverse, parishes affirm the impression of their attitude toward modesty and simplicity in relation to holy places in which spiritual power lives.

Imagery of a Shared Belief

In any large city in the American and Canadian Pacific Northwest, there are quite a few indigenous art objects in the most central locations. It is a landmark of this area that identifies with these symbols of presence and respect for the culture of the indigenous peoples of the region. But what is the additional value of these art objects, what message do they carry?

Among the items on sale at the Washington State Legislature gift shop in Olympia, Washington, the author's attention was drawn to a children's coloring book about nature and society, based on the symbols of indigenous art, published in Vancouver, British Columbia [51]. Each page of the book contains drawings of one or another animal or other living and non-living objects of nature (for example, the Moon and the Sun), gradually leading to ideas about who lives in the Sky and in the Ocean, who is big and who is small, as well as direct ecological concepts such as the Respect: Reduce, Reuse, Recycle page (Fig. 29).

Reduce   Reuse   Recycle

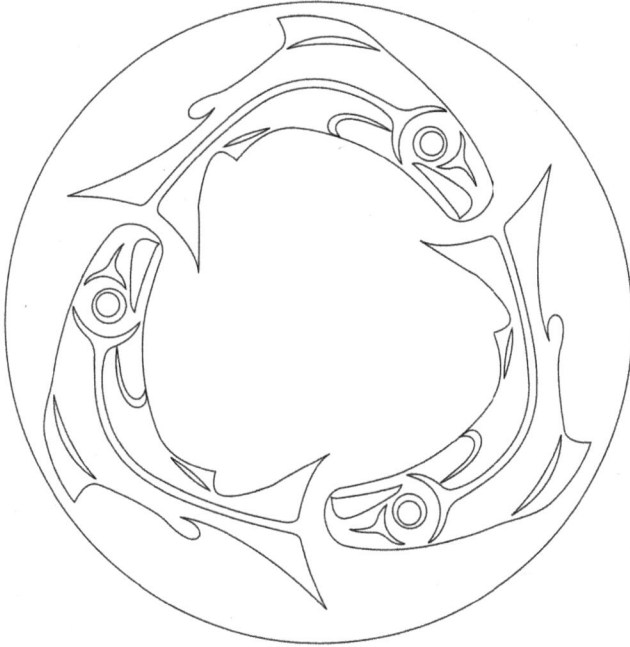

R E S P E C T

__educe   __euse   __ecycle

Use green to colour the salmon
Print the missing letter for each word

Figure 29. *Pacific Northwest Indigenous Art Activity Book*, Vancouver, BC: Native Northwest, 2021, p. 13.

In the foreword to the book, Simone Diamond, a Salish Coast artist, puts it this way:

Our traditional art embodies our rich history and way of living in the natural and supernatural world. These connections have been central to who we are as a people and continue to offer us strength and foster resilience. Our ancestors have passed down their knowledge for thousands of years. As a mother and an artist, it is important for me that my daughter learns about our art, culture, and the history of our family so she can continue this legacy.

There are numerous Indigenous cultures in the Pacific Northwest. While each is unique, they share many similarities: we value the land, we value our ancestors, and we value our traditions. It is critical that we all, as parents and as a community, pass down our knowledge to our children [51, Foreword].

The message of indigenous art in the cities of the region, as well as the use of local art symbols for educational purposes, suggests that environmental thinking as a policy, education, and even religion in the Pacific Northwest is largely based on and influenced by the worldviews of indigenous people. Statistics showing that British Columbia, Washington, and Oregon have the highest percentage of atheist populations fail to take into account that the vast majority of these "atheists" are people whose religious views transcend historical religions and approach ecology as a religion of shared responsibility for our future on this planet.

Part II
MUSIC IN THE CHURCH

Chapter 4

Historical and Local Tunes in Hymnbooks

Since about the early 1990s, national hymnbooks around the world have included musical material, some of which may seem unrelated not only to the musical traditions of the communities but, more broadly, to the public's national heritage [52, p. 24]. The question arises as to what was the reason for going beyond national/confessional boundaries in the choice of music and what this issue tells us about the global sociocultural processes in the modern world. Another question concerns the components of group identity and their balance, namely the "religious" part of national identity and the "national" part of religious identity. Regarding such regions as the Pacific Northwest, this is a vital rather than a theoretical question, and it sheds light on the multicultural mechanism of modern Canadian and American society, especially on the West Coast. H. S. Donaldson, who has studied the hymnals published by the major Protestant churches in Canada since the eve of the twentieth century, puts it this way:

Land, Faith, and Voice: Christian Music in the Pacific Northwest
Alexander Rosenblatt
Copyright © 2024 Jenny Stanford Publishing Pte. Ltd.
ISBN 978-981-5129-11-3 (Hardcover), 978-1-003-47332-9 (eBook)
www.jennystanford.com

Why should Canadians sing cross-culturally? A country that has often been called a cultural mosaic, Canada is home to voices from multiple cultural contexts which often live and work alongside one another. This mosaic encompasses the many cultures of the world which call Canada home, as well as the rich heritage of indigenous Canadians [3, p. 18].

There are also other factors and circumstances that determine the further movement toward cultural diversity in the various hymnbooks that one has to deal with when visiting different churches in the study area. That is, figuratively speaking, if you are traveling to the Pacific Northwest with a pocket edition of the hymnal used in your home church, and you intend to use the book while visiting churches of the same denomination there, it is unlikely that the churches you attend use the same book.

Hymnbooks and Sociocultural Agenda

As mentioned above in Chapter 2, the split in all Protestant churches in the United States and Canada, most clearly manifested in the Pacific Northwest as the most "atheistic" region of the continent, caused the appearance of a variety of hymnal books published or associated with these churches in one way or another. In addition to the evangelical/mainline divide within each individual white Protestant denomination, the likelihood of finding one or another book available to this community in a particular church is also influenced by the personal stance of every single clergyperson. As a result, you can hardly predict what hymnbook you will find on the pew of an Episcopalian, Methodist, United, Presbyterian, or any other local Protestant church in Victoria and Vancouver (BC), Seattle, or Portland (OR). One more thing to consider when discussing the hymnbooks accepted in each individual church is their ethnic composition. Churches with predominantly Chinese, Korean, or Hispanic congregations not only hold services in those languages but also use hymnal books published in their respective countries. Depending on the musical background and preferences of the priest and the musical style adopted in each place, a separate sheet of music or sheet music printed on a service leaflet can be offered at the entrance to the church or found on a pew.

The Catholic churches appear to be a single entity from both a hierarchical and theological point of view. There is no open discussion of any controversial points. However, two historical events have directly affected the quality of musical selections currently found in several hymnal books, associated with the Catholic service in the United States and Canada in general and the Pacific Northwest in particular. The first such event was an instruction issued by Pope Pius X in 1903, which clearly stated that "the more closely a composition for church approaches in its movement, inspiration and savor the Gregorian form, the more sacred and liturgical it becomes" [53]. The implication of this gesture was that the Catholic Church no longer encouraged composers to write new compositions of liturgical content if they were not based on medieval (or reminiscent of medieval) melodies. Thus, the Catholic Church was clearly retreating to the era of modal monophony. The second event was the Second Vatican Council (1962–1965), which legalized Catholic service in vernacular languages and encouraged congregational singing during mass rather than "singing the mass," that is, the traditional texts of the Eucharist. In the United States and Canada, this directive has been interpreted as permission to introduce hymn singing into the practice of Catholic communities, as is done in Protestant churches, to ensure that the former are "musically competitive" with the latter.

The Hymn: Historical Reference

The oldest musical item of the Christian service, the hymn seems to be the most ambiguous genre of those sung in the church. At various times, hymns were completely ignored, or, conversely, completely substituted the other liturgical genres. The extreme flexibility of this early liturgical genre is due to its starting point as a non-dogmatic song of praise to God. The hymn might be distinguished by two important and consistent features: (1) a metrical structure of both music and text and (2) its convenience for congregational singing. The metrical structure of a hymn is determined by the rules of classical Latin versification. Correspondence between music and words in hymns is flexible: different texts with the same meter may be sung to the same melody. Hymnals (hymnbooks) have usually included an index grouping the hymns according to their poetic meters in order to facilitate their setting to a proper melody.

Hymns and Related Non-dogmatic Genres

From the beginning, hymns were differentiated from Psalms. The development of hymnody was linked to the use of rhythmical prose in the early church. The use of hymns in the Eastern Church reached a peak in the fourth century. Since then, only single-stanza hymns (troparia) might be found in service books. The Roman Catholic Church admitted hymns in the twelfth century, but only in 1963 was the congregational use of "religious songs" encouraged by the Second Vatican Council. Protestant hymns, from their very beginning, differed from the Catholic ones in that they were sung by the laity.

The first appearance of Christian hymns in English dates back to the eighth century. In the late Middle Ages, a specifically English form of hymn—the Carol—was developed. An attempt to bring Lutheran chorales (hymns) into the English service did not succeed, and hymns disappeared from service books as they were superseded by metrical versions of the Psalter (as in Calvinist France).

For a variety of reasons, the hymns came back to the Church of England in the nineteenth century. On American soil, where the Church of England (in the United States—Episcopal Church) encountered a vast Afro-American laity, an autochthonous form of Christian hymn developed, the so-called *Negro spirituals*. Most of the English-speaking churches in the world adopted the hymn as an integral part of worship (rather than an addition to it).

Missionaries, who work with indigenous communities in the Pacific Northwest,

> [...] believed that hymns were one of the best tools to stir Indigenous minds into accepting Christianity and the habits of civilized and morally "upstanding" lives. Drawing on contemporary educational theory, which held that hymn singing to children was an effective tool of pedagogy, missionaries composed hymns intended to inculcate Christian beliefs and "civilized" habits amongst Indigenous people [47, p. 29].

Hymnbooks became the main (if not the only) written musical source for use in the Protestant mass toward the end of the second millennium. These hymnals often comprise other musical forms besides hymns that are essential for the service. Thus, the *New English Hymnal* (1994), for example, includes a liturgical section that "supplies two simple settings for the Eucharist," one by John Merbecke (c1505–c1585), and a second one, "a new congregational setting in speech-rhythm" [54, p. vi], for the Alternative Service Book (1980), a regulating document that offers a wide choice of language and liturgy to each Anglican church.

The Place of Hymns in the Liturgy

Whereas in Western liturgy, a hymn was always a kind of sideshow, it was given a new breath at the juncture of the nineteenth and twentieth centuries. "Art music" of the era became less listenable to an average parishioner, and church authorities became quite sensitive on this point. Thus, issued on the eve of World War I, the Catholic Encyclopedia held that "High Mass is not the music but the deacon and subdeacon" [55, p. 799]. This statement clearly indicates that in the early twentieth century, the Western Church had become so critical to music that it was willing to give it up, rather than let the music set the ceremony.

This situation lasted for decades, and hymns in the meantime became an ideal solution for the church fathers to stay afloat in the turbulent waters of changing tastes and trends. Still, as noted much later,

[t]he serious composer of church music today has to wrestle with the difficulty of finding a way to write a hymn tune in an idiom that is not only legitimate and contemporary but also valid. In a word, his tune must be suitable for congregational use. To retrace the well-worn paths of earlier styles is much easier, no doubt, but he who does this loses his own identity [56, p. (v)].

Although from about the early 1960s, new styles of song— primarily various forms of church pop and rock music, including worship songs—replaced traditional hymns for a time in much of the English-language Protestant ministry, they gradually made a comeback as the 1990s approached.

For various reasons, the missionary work, and then the post-missionary reconfiguration of churches and local parishes—all this spiritual, educational, and organizational enterprise was possible only thanks to the ecumenical position of missionaries and local clergy. A striking example of this is the Anglican-Lutheran bishopric in Jerusalem (founded in 1841), which lasted for about 40 years, before splitting into two churches [57, Ch. 3]. In the same way, the non-dogmatic character of the hymn allowed the joint committees to abstain from doctrinal or theological differences between churches and to produce hymnbooks, shared by several denominations and therefore perceived as rather national collections of church music. Thus, the Preface to the *Hymnal Book* (1971), a joint publication of the two Protestant churches, clearly states that "nothing in this Hymn Book is of any authority on matters relating to faith or doctrine in the Anglican Church of Canada or the United Church of Canada" [56, p. (iv)]. However, as recently noted, this book appeared to be "too Anglican for the Uniteds and too United for the Anglicans" [3, p. 19].

Churches and Hymnbooks

In most churches associated with Western Christianity, hymnbooks with printed music became the only source for congregational singing. The release of modified books every three decades or so is perceived as an event and a message to society from the fathers of the church. The heritage of the Western Church musical tradition (in its historical depth), modern praise and worship songs, melodies representing different musical cultures of the world, and, finally, local folk melodies that are in every collection of hymns—all this is a kind of historical and cultural message for parishioners, while the different sociocultural and theological agendas of the clergy of the same denomination often result in the use of different hymnbooks for ministry in their churches.

Books of the Protestant Churches

Folk and popular music have often been an integral part of Christian service at various points in history. In the fifteenth century, for example, composers used melodies of secular songs as *cantus firmus* in the tenor line of the polyphonic mass. Since the Renaissance these processes accelerated, and each period brought into the church— the Catholic one and most especially the Reform—elements of the contemporary folk and popular music cultures drawn from the secular public spaces outside the church [58]. This interaction and the use of common sonic baggage between the church and the secular environment has become one of the indirect, albeit the most obvious markers of the decentralization of religion in Western society.

The twentieth century, however, introduced a further revolutionary challenge to Western Church music (in particular, Anglican music), as it experienced the unprecedented expansion into the church of the pop-rock style of music. By the 1950s, the Anglican musical establishment made a new attempt to adopt music "in a popular style specifically for Sunday worship, striking at the heart of the English hymn and choral tradition" [59, p. 431]. This new style included "a variety of different genres under the heading of 'church pop' [with] some common qualities between them" [59, p. 432]. The glorious heritage of English hymnody was at risk of being superseded by new pop-rock-inspired praise songs. The hymn, however, has stood the test of time and remains the main genre of Protestant, including Anglican, worship to this day.

While the Catholic Church was retreating toward medieval melodies, the connection between living composers and Protestant church music practices continued in search of the proper path. The language of musical modernism could not have been appropriate. As Clarke notes, "twentieth-century 'art-music' idioms are not generally understood or liked in church congregations. It is doubtful that congregations would ever try to sing atonal hymn tunes" [60, p. 153]. Yet, as noted in the introduction to a hymnal of the late 1930s: "[e]ach generation, with its problems and outlook, must ever seek ways of expressing its ideas and aspirations." (61, p. iii). The preface to a later collection of hymns is even more specific: "Young people especially wish to sing hymns cast in the style of the twentieth century" [56, p. (iv)]. This clearly refers to the pop-rock music of that period.

It appears that the last editions of the hymnals before the split of the Protestant churches throughout the United States and Canada were published during the 1990s and are still in use today. The fact is that some churches—especially those that have moved (or stayed) to an evangelical agenda—have "jumped" to using hymnal books from other places (such as Kenya or Rwanda), where the books have kept a clear conservative line in terms of delicate values and issues.

As of this writing, updated hymnbooks have not been published by Protestant churches of any denomination or division in either the United States or Canada. However, there are strong indications that new hymnbooks, whether a supplement to the existing latest hymnbook (e.g., *Sing a New Creation* by the Anglican Church of Canada), or an expanded edition of the classic hymnbook (from the United Evangelical Church) are being prepared for release.

In the statistics and analysis section later in this chapter, we will look at two Protestant hymnbooks, one published by a particular church, and the other—a bilingual hymnal (in Chinese and English) intended for use by various Protestant denominations, which, in particular, serves as a hymnbook at the Anglican Missionary Church in Richmond, British Columbia, Canada.

Books of the Catholic Churches

Although the Catholic Church has not been subject to division on the basis of liberal or conservative trends, still the various English-language hymnbooks—all intended for use in the Catholic Church—and the subsequent revised editions of these books testify to the different approaches to various issues of the Catholic agenda, which tries to keep up with the times.

The two aforementioned conflicting directives—to follow the medieval modal monophony (1903) and to allow congregational singing of accompanied hymns (1963)—were supplemented by questions of choral polyphony, the inclusion of hymns of Protestant origin and folk melodies of different peoples in hymnbooks, as well as questions of linguistic style in canonical and extra-liturgical texts. As a result, the presence of this or that hymnal (in place of or in addition to the Missal) on the pew is as unpredictable as in Protestant churches. A brief description of the differences between the four subsequent editions of *Worship* by GIA Publications and the two editions of *The Adoremus Hymnal* by Ignatius Press outlines the differences in approaches mentioned.

Any edition of *Worship* is a hymnal and service book (Missal) at the same time. For the first time, the book was published in 1971, and it introduced congregational singing typical of Protestant churches in Roman Catholic service in the U.S. Second edition (1975) already restores the old-style "thee" and "thy" in hymn lyrics, instead of "you" and "your" [45, p. (ii)]. Yet, the book still begins with hymns, followed by a liturgical section. The third edition (1986) reorders the book, which now opens with a liturgical section (followed by hymns), thus presenting "who we are and how we pray as Roman Catholics within the larger Christian community" [62, p. (i)]. The fourth edition (2011) is again more diverse and multicultural than the previous one but in a slightly different way. It contains several titles from the repertoire of church songs with piano/guitar accompaniment. Hymns and songs in Spanish are included "to recognize, in a small way, the increasingly multicultural nature of many assemblies" [63, p. (ii)]. Songs from the Taizé sources, the ecclesiastical legacy of medieval chants, church and folk melodies from many nations, as well as a significant presence of hymns and songs by living American composers are part of this collection. Unlike the three previous editions, the fourth edition has pew and choral versions.

Churches in the Pacific Northwest have different responses to the changes between the editions. Thus, St. James Cathedral in Seattle, as of 2021, still uses the second edition as its pew hymnal.

Catholic churches, which take a more conservative line in terms of musical similarities to Protestant services, use different books for the regular portions of mass and the singing of hymns. As such a couple, *Lumen Christi Missal* from Illuminare Publications, in which every melody is printed according to medieval neumatic notation in four lines, and the second edition (2011) of *The Adoremus Hymnal* [64] could be considered. You will find these two books, for example, on the pew of the Proto-Cathedral of St. James in Vancouver, Washington. Latin mass at this church is one of only six places permitted for Latin services in Oregon and Washington. Latin language service is not available in British Columbia.

The Adoremus Hymnal (2011) contains mass settings (in the medieval notation for the Latin text on every even-numbered page, and in the modern notation for the English text to the same melody on every corresponding odd page) and a hymnal section which is, however, much less varied than in the fourth edition of *Worship* published the same year. The second edition of *Adoremus* has a Standard edition featuring the hymnal in full harmonization (for parishioners and choir), the Melody (Pew) edition, and the Organ edition.

Hymnbooks at Comparison

Since the musical collections found in the hymnals represent the position of the church at a particular time, a comparison of the hymnbooks issued over the course of one decade for different local denominations of the same church may contribute to a better understanding of the direction in which modern Christianity is moving. The comparison of hymnbooks will be carried out with an emphasis on the historical scope and geographical coverage of musical selections, presented in each particular book. Yet, there will be additional points of reference, which directly or indirectly contribute to the same subject, such as the modal framework of musical selections throughout a book, the use of historical forms of notation, or the accompaniment style for plainsongs. The comparison will be between two selected hymnbooks used by the English- and Chinese-speaking Anglican communities of Greater Vancouver (BC, Canada) respectively, both published in the late 1990s (latest available to date):

Common Praise. Toronto: Anglican Book Centre, 1998 [65]
(hereafter: The Canadian book) and
Hymns of Universal Praise. Hong Kong: Chinese Christian Literature
Council, 1996 [66]
(hereafter: The Chinese book),

and recent editions of the two aforementioned American Catholic hymnbooks:

The Adoremus Hymnal, Second Edition. San Francisco, CA: Ignatus
Press, 2011 [64]
(hereafter: The Adoremus) and
Worship, Fourth edition. Chicago, IL: GIA Publications, 2011 [63]
(hereafter: Worship IV).

We will also refer to earlier editions of these books and other related books such as *English Hymnal* (1994) by Canterbury Press (UK) [54].

Historical and Geographical Coverage

Attribution of the melodies appears in each specific collection of hymns, although it follows slightly different terminology and methods of distinction. While the earliest melodies, whose origins are rather vague, appear everywhere under the name "plainsong" or "Gregorian chant," or just provided with the number of the church mode, as in Worship IV. Tunes taken from an early psalter or hymnal can appear under the name of this collection if there is no other information about the source. National melodies, in addition to the heading denoting nationality, usually receive an extension providing further information, for example, traditional, folk, hymn, carol, or church melody. While the information about authors and sources normally are presented in different lists for texts and music, the Canadian book offers a unified index of authors and sources for both texts and music. Whatever the nuances in terminology and methods of indexing, the very tendency for accuracy in attribution attests to the intention of the compilers to highlight the historical scale of a particular collection and its cultural diversity (or, conversely, cultural unity when one culture is represented in many varieties). The historical scope and geographical coverage of the four hymnbooks compared are shown in Chart 1.

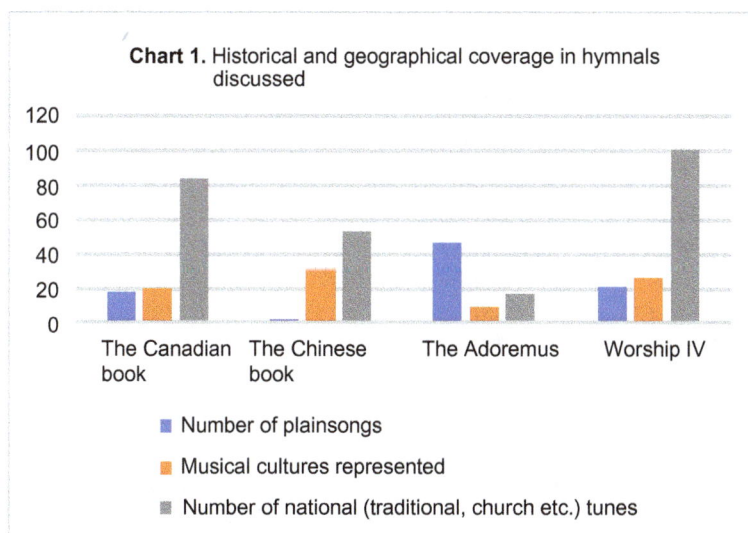

Chart 1. Historical and geographical coverage in hymnals discussed

The number of musical selections varies from book to book, and we cannot calculate them accurately since the body of the hymnody is followed (or preceded) by the sections of various settings, including morning and evening prayers. For statistical purposes, I am only referring to the estimated number of hymns in each book. The number of hymns in three of the four books is quite close: the Canadian book contains 665, the Chinese book—663, and Worship IV—613 hymns. The Adoremus shows a much smaller number, only 190 hymns, while the range of their serial numbers (from 300 to 636) has many gaps with missing numbers preserved for an as-yet unpublished extended version of the book. In terms of the number of represented national cultures, the Chinese book holds a leading position—32 geographic locations, considering both traditional and sacred national tunes. Worship IV with 26 locations leads in the number of melodies associated with different national cultures—101 such melodies. The Adoremus, rather modest in terms of representing national musical cultures (only 17 traditional melodies), contains a significant number of early medieval chants—46 plainsongs versus about 20 in the Canadian book and Worship IV. The Canadian book pays special attention to the country's indigenous languages—12 of the 18 languages other than English featured in the book (the other three books contain only one or two additional languages, including Latin).

Hymns and songs written by contemporary and local composers are highly indicative of editorial research and contributions to each collection. While the Adoremus contains only 13 melodies written after 1900, including three American authors whose life dates are incorrect or missing (!?), and the Canadian book contains 36 melodies written by four local (i.e., Canadian) composers, the selection of local American composers in Worship IV is impressive in its abundance—20 hymns by 12 American composers of the 19th century and 139 hymns/songs by 50 American composers of the 20th century or living composers (see Chart 2).

While Healey Willan (1880–1968), a British-Canadian composer, is featured in the Canadian book with 13 arrangements and original compositions, and Ralph Vaughan Williams (1872–1958), a British church music composer, is heavily featured in Worship IV, the undisputed authority in the collections of all denominations is Jacques Berthier (1923–1994), a French composer of liturgical music, mainly known for writing most of the music used by the Taizé community. The books also contain music written by composers born, active, or living in the Pacific Northwest. Along with Healey

Willan, these are Patrick Wedd, Rupert Lang, and Bob Hurd. The contributions of these and some other composers to the church music of the Pacific Northwest will be discussed later in Chapters 5 and 6.

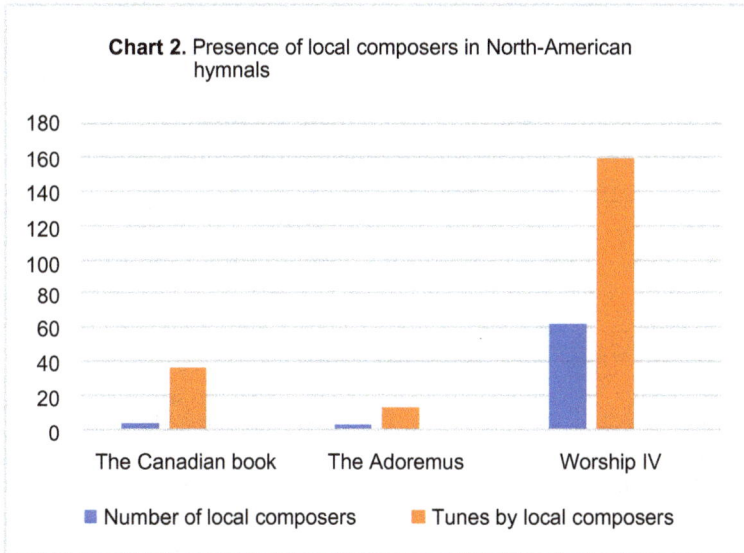

Chart 2. Presence of local composers in North-American hymnals

Normally, the balance between the major and minor keys throughout a hymnbook is about 75 percent to 25 percent. This historically proven proportion can be found in most hymnbooks, both Catholic and Protestant, including the Canadian book, the Adoremus, Worship IV, *English Hymnal*, and two editions (1940 and 1982) of *The Hymnal* for the Episcopal Church in the United States [67, 68]. The Chinese book, however, shows a different balance: 90 percent of the tunes are in a major key and 10 percent of the tunes are in a minor key. This balance can also be found in some other post-missionary hymnbooks produced in various places, such as the Middle East, where the local musical culture is more favorable to major Western modes/keys than to minor ones [52, pp. 32–33].

Forms of Notation

Different hymnals offer different notations for medieval church tunes. Thus, the Adoremus offers a historical notation as attractive with its superior graphic design as it is illegible not only for parishioners but also for an experienced musician (see Example 1).

Example 1. *Kyrie* as appears in the "Ordinaries" section of the Adoremus.

126 KYRIE

The other tune for *Kyrie* in the Adoremus (from the canonized "Mass VI") is far more readable. In Worship IV, the same tune is given in modern notation being transposed a tone down (see Examples 2a and b).

Example 2. *Kyrie* from Mass VI as printed:

MASS XVI

℣. *Ký-ri-e,* *e-lé-i-son.* ℟. **Ký-ri-e,** **e-lé-i-son.**

℣. *Christe,* *e-lé-i-son.* ℟. **Christe,** **e-lé-i-son.**

℣. *Ký-ri-e,* *e-lé-i-son.* ℟. **Ký-ri-e,** **e-lé-i-son. vel** ... **e-lé-i-son.**

(a) in the "Order of the Mass" section of the Adoremus, p. 16.

340 **KYRIE**

ed. Vat. XVI
Acc. by Gerard Farrell. OSB, 1985

Ky - ri - e, e - le - i - son. Ky - ri - e, e - le - i - son.

Chri - ste, e - le - i - son. Chri - ste, e - le - i - son. Ky - ri -

e, e - le - i - son. Ky - ri - e, e - le - i - son.

(b) in the liturgical section of Worship IV.

Example 3. Special/historical forms of notation throughout the hymnbooks:

A - men. Al - le - lu - ia.

(a) neumatic notation supplemented by modern one (*English Hymnal*).

Glo - ry to you for - ev - er and ev - er.

(b) two-line notation (the Canadian book).

1. 亞 伯 拉 罕 的 土, 高 處 施 行 統 治,
2. 高 處 居 住 君 王: 正 直, 善 義, 公 平,

(c) numeric notation (the Chinese book).

English Hymnal represents two forms of musical notation for each plainsong: historic (neumatic) and modern notation, accompanied by modal harmony. The Canadian book presents most of the plainsongs in modern notation with modal harmony. Unaccompanied plainsong melodies in this book receive a two-line notation, also typical of some American (Protestant) hymnals. Church modes of the plainsongs are indicated in all the books under discussion. Pentatonic scales are part of the regional traditional melodies in the Chinese book, which offers numeric notation (in addition to modern notation) for all melodies with Chinese text in this bilingual book. The forms of notation typical for each of the books mentioned are shown in Example 3a–c.

The Qualities of Musical Selections

What determines the musical choices for the hymnbook? What are the reasons for this or that expansion of historical scale, geographic coverage, or both? In addition to the original value as the only source for congregational singing, the hymnals of the 1990s onward perform additional functions, such as the unification of an ethnic group or even a nation, especially when the self-identification of a group or person is based on the native language and cultural tradition rather than on the place of birth. Thus, 13 Chinese melodies in the Chinese book serve their target audience regardless of the location of a particular Chinese-speaking parish.

Musical choice can also seem a kind of political gesture. Such are, for example, two Taiwanese melodies in the Chinese book— the *Ping-pu* folk song and the *Tayal* folk song. The inclusion of two folk melodies from Taiwan in the Chinese collection of hymns may seem like a musical reminder of the tragic pages in the relationship between the Republic of China and Taiwan. Another example of a socio-political gesture of such kind is the inclusion of hymns in 12 languages of the First Nations (that is, indigenous peoples of Canada) in the Canadian book, although the book does not include melodies associated with these demographic groups. The openness of the editors of these books, as well as of Worship IV, to the Hebrew and Orthodox melodies attests to the ecumenical tendency typical for post-missionary churches in the global era.

As the review shows, the musical selections of the books discussed in this chapter reflect many musical cultures, whether it be the historical heritage of the Western Church, local musical culture, or other cultures in close or distant circles of the target audience. Different musical cultures are represented in each hymnbook in various notation forms and with appropriate harmony (if applicable). Early forms of notation are present in every hymnal, lending depth and flavor to the historical retrospective.

Ecumenism and Sociocultural Narrative

The ecumenical trend, typical of post-missionary churches in the global age, prompted the editorial search and release of hymnal books in such a way that it was often a collaborative effort between two or more missionary churches. As a result, some of these hymnals have a national rather than confessional value. Much attention has been paid, in particular, to the post-missionary reconfiguration of the communities, taking into account the way plainsongs, local and various folk melodies are presented in national hymnal books, as well as the balance (in each particular collection) between major and minor scales, and the convenience of congregational singing.

Compared to other sources of church music, hymnal books often contain deeper historical and wider geographical coverage; they also feature extensively local motives and external musical "blotches" as a tribute to other cultures. Since they belong to the church and not to civil society, national hymnbooks have become, albeit indirect, but still a reliable source to outline the socio-cultural narrative of certain peoples and localities in a certain period.

As the main and sometimes the only source of music sung in the church, the hymnbooks found in the churches of the studied area provide basic information about the attendee's expectations in this regard. Yet, what actually happens, in terms of music, in the churches of the Pacific Northwest during prayers, community gatherings, and other extra-liturgical events?

Chapter 5

Musical Practices in Cathedrals and Parish Churches

Divine services (that is, the Eucharistic mass, morning and evening prayers) as well as various paraliturgical and extra-liturgical events in different churches of the Pacific Northwest occur in a fairly diverse (traditional, modern, local, or mixed) form. Depending on, and sometimes irrespective of, the rank of a particular church, cathedrals and parish churches throughout British Columbia, Washington, and Oregon represent vastly different musical frameworks and practices. Below we turn to the palette of regional church music, looking at the weekly Eucharistic services, other divine services, festivals of church music, concerts, and a variety of community gatherings accompanied by singing.

Northwestern Eucharist

Regular services with music on a weekly basis (some on a monthly basis) include events and elements as varied in style and origin as choral Evensong, Taizé music, indigenous songs, a children's choir,

Land, Faith, and Voice: Christian Music in the Pacific Northwest
Alexander Rosenblatt
Copyright © 2024 Jenny Stanford Publishing Pte. Ltd.
ISBN 978-981-5129-11-3 (Hardcover), 978-1-003-47332-9 (eBook)
www.jennystanford.com

and a professional choir performing a wide repertoire in churches of Greater Vancouver and Victoria (British Columbia), Seattle and Vancouver (Washington), and Portland (Oregon). Let's start the discussion with the elements of the musical part of the Eucharistic liturgy.

Catholic churches, and even more so cathedrals, represent two trends existing in modern Catholicism, one of which strictly follows the directive of Pius X (1903) to use only Gregorian chants in the liturgy, and the second expands the repertoire of historical chants with music more related to the approval of congregational singing by Vatican II (1963). A striking example of this dichotomy is the musical solutions of the two cathedrals in Washington State. Thus, the music of the Sunday Eucharistic service in the Catholic Cathedral of St. James in Seattle includes many sung parts, the music for which (in various, including modal, styles) was written in the 20th century. That is, the treasure of the wealth of church music of the 17th–19th centuries (mainly against which the Pope fought) is still abandoned. Example 4 shows some of the titles of the Ordinary parts sung there during the mass on the Twenty-Second Sunday, August 29, 2021.

When attending a Sunday service at the Proto-Cathedral of St. James in Vancouver, Washington, you will hear only three or four hymns, each based on modal Gregorian chants, which effectively corresponds to Pius X's directive regarding the only authorized source of church music but, in fact, also to the Vatican II, which encouraged congregational singing. So, the above trends do not seem to be in direct conflict.

Protestant churches (regardless of the theological/ideological division) represent a greater variety of styles and epochs represented in the musical part of the Eucharistic mass in each church. Churches of the Anglican-Episcopal affiliation represent, perhaps, the richest musical collection, not limited by directives that ban part of the musical heritage of the Western Church. Some of the churches, such as Christ Church Cathedral, Victoria, British Columbia, have offered such a special (for this region) historical form of the main church service as the Celtic Eucharist with its own musical arrangement. To date, the tradition, which ceased during the COVID-19 pandemic, has not been resumed until the time of this writing.

Example 4. Leaflet of the Sunday mass at St. James' Catholic Cathedral, Seattle, Washington, August 29, 2021, p. iii.

GLORIA   *Mass in Honor of St. Benedict*
                                                          Robert LeBlanc (b. 1948)

Glo - ry to God in the high - est, and on earth peace to peo - ple of good will. We

praise you, we bless you, we a - dore you, we glo - ri - fy you, we give you thanks for

your great glo - ry, Lord God heav - en - ly King, O God, al - might - y Fa - ther.

Cantor or Choir:
Lord Jesus Christ, Only Begotten Son, Lord God, Lamb of God, Son of the Father, you take away the sins of the world, have mercy on us; you take away the sins of the world, receive our prayer; you are seated at the right hand of the Father, have mercy on us.

For you a - lone are the Ho - ly One, you a - lone are the Lord,

you a - lone are the Most High, Je - sus Christ, with the Ho - ly Spir - it, in the

glo - ry of God the Fa - ther. A - men, a - men, a - - - men.

COLLECT (OPENING PRAYER)

The Liturgy of the Word

FIRST READING   Deuteronomy 4:1-2, 6-8
RESPONSORIAL PSALM   Psalm 15
                                                          Richard Proulx (1938–2010)

Those who do jus - tice will live in the pres - ence of the Lord.

SECOND READING   James 1:17-18, 21b-22, 27
ALLELUIA   Jacques Berthier (1923–1994)

Al - le - lu - ia, al - le - lu - ia, al - le - lu - ia.

Al - le - lu - ia, al - le - lu - ia, al - le - lu - ia!

The music scene at St. James Anglican Church and Christ Church Cathedral, both in Vancouver, British Columbia, is a sort of competition between the oldest denominational church in the city and its current central church. However, the old church tends to use modal melodies, historical or composed in the 20th century, such as those by H. Willan, during the regular Sunday service, while the cathedral places more emphasis on modern compositions, such as the works of R. G. Lang—compare Examples 5 and 6. (The music of both these musicians, as well as some other modern American and Canadian composers, especially those from the Pacific Northwest, will be discussed in Chapter 6.)

Example 5. Leaflet of the High Mass at St. James' Anglican Church, Vancouver, British Columbia, October 27, 2013, p. 6.

INTROIT

Let the hearts of those who seek the Lord rejoice. Look to the Lord your God, and he will strengthen you; do not cease to seek his face. *Psalm* Give thanks to the Lord, and call upon his Name: make known his deeds among the peoples. Remember the marvels he has done: his wonders and the judgments of his mouth.

Laetetur cor (Mode II)

KYRIE ELEISON

Setting: *Missa de Sancta Maria Magdalena* - Healey Willan (1880-1968)

At holyday masses, both churches, and even more so the church of St. James, offer musical solutions in which "art music" of the 19th century presents the *Ordinary* parts with the *Proper* part from early sources. "Music aspires to express what is otherwise inexpressible," reads the web page of St. James' High Mass Choir. "For this reason, music is integral to our liturgies at St. James'. We draw on the rich musical heritage of the Western Church, from its roots in plainsong to the finest music of our time" [69].

Music in parish churches is simpler and does not follow High Mass standards and patterns. However, opening and closing organ preludes (sometimes called "voluntaries") are part of almost any

Protestant Sunday mass. Such are works by Bach, composers of the Classical and Romantic eras, or modern composers, including organ works by H. Willan.

Example 6.   "Kyrie" from the *Mass for Many Nations* by R. G. Lang as printed at the leaflet of Christ Church Cathedral, Vancouver, BC, November 24, 2013, p. 4.

Praise songs, as a relatively new part of the musical arrangement in Protestant churches, are presented in both evangelical and mainline wings of the churches, but to a greater extent in the evangelical ones, which take into account the traditional musical environment of each particular Protestant denomination somewhat less. These songs are written in a fairly traditional style, associated with the modern mass or youth musical tradition of the homeland of a particular parish. Thus, the Chinese community will sing praise songs in Mandarin or Cantonese, Korean Protestants in Korean, and the native English-speaking community will sing "church rock" songs in English. Usually, the Sunday service begins with two songs of praise, and two others are sung toward the end of the service. The festive mass may include more of these songs.

The music of the Mass in churches where the majority of the congregation are not native English speakers may incorporate musical instruments typical of the congregants' country of origin. Thus, congregants originating in Mexico may use instruments rather uncommon in a North American church service, such as the natural scale xylophone in one of the Anglican churches in New Westminster, British Columbia (Fig. 30).

Figure 30. Mexican xylophone at St. Barnabas Church, New Westminster, BC. Photo by the author, 2013.

Regional indigenous churches of any Christian denomination (that is, of their own, like the Indian Shaker Church, or those established by missionaries) may maintain their own musical patterns regardless of denominational belonging. Thus, the Indian Shaker Church in Duncan (Vancouver Island), BC, holds settings of the songs typical of the Suquamish and Duwamish traditions that accompany every main service in this church.

Evening Prayers

Among worship services other than the Eucharistic mass, the most musically enhanced divine services in the major churches of various denominations of the Western Church throughout the Pacific Northwest are evening prayers—the weekly (sometimes monthly) choir Evensong (vespers) or Compline during which various layers of plainsong and unaccompanied polyphony of the Baroque era are performed by a male, female, or mixed choir. Such prayers attract the attention not only of the parishioners of a particular church but also of many guests of the city, who plan their stay taking into account visiting one or another place where the tradition is preserved.

As a rule, the leading cathedrals of any city in the study area advertise their musical solutions for various liturgical and non-liturgical services and events, including weekday and evening hours, so that people planning a trip to a particular city can choose a service or other event that they can visit at a convenient time in a particular church, largely depending on their musical preferences. Given that music can play a critical role here, church leaders are focusing on promoting music solutions in their churches by hosting a church choir/church music page on their website. For example, Trinity Episcopal Cathedral in Portland, Oregon defines the musical range under its umbrella as follows:

> Music at Trinity Cathedral is diverse, creative, and grounded in the unique Anglican heritage of music in the Episcopal Church. Our music reflects the variety and scope of our Cathedral liturgies, from the regular Sunday morning Eucharist to reflective Evensong services and brilliant festive occasions to world-class concerts and recitals featuring musicians from across the globe [70].

Up until the COVID-19 pandemic, two of Vancouver, BC's oldest Anglican churches, St. James' Church and Christ Church Cathedral, both part of the Mainline division, offered their musically enhanced evening prayers (Evensong and Compline, respectively), during which various works by finest English composers of the past, Thomas Tallis, William Byrd, and Orlando Gibbons, were performed by a four-part ensemble and church choir, a cappella or accompanied.

In contrast to this historically reconstructed musical tradition, St. John's Church in Vancouver, affiliated with the evangelical division of the Canadian Anglicans, held evening services that included only contemporary praise songs. Being quite conservative in terms of its attitude to the modern trends of a liberal society, this church offers less traditional solutions both in music and in the clothes of its clergy.

St. James Cathedral (Catholic) in Seattle maintains Ecumenical Prayer in the form of music from Taizé communities. Such an event was held, for example, on May 1, 2020, when the cathedral guitarist M. H. Wilson performed a program of guitar (and arranged for guitar) music from different centuries called "Joy" (Fig. 31).

✠ ST. JAMES CATHEDRAL ✠ SEATTLE ✠ 1 MAY 2020 ✠ 6:30 PM ✠

MUSICAL PRAYER

MARK HILLIARD WILSON

St. James Cathedral Guitarist

"JOY"

Ode to Joy from *Symphony No. 9*, op. 125	Ludwig van Beethoven
	1770–1827
arr. Mark Hilliard Wilson from an arrangement for organ by Nuno Carmona	
All creatures of our God and King	William Henry Draper
	1855–1933
Choro Gavotte from *Suite Populaire Brésilienne*	Heitor Villa-Lobos
	1908–1992
Liebesbotschaft from *Schwanengesang*, D.957	Franz Schubert
(*"Message of Love"*)	1797–1828
	arr. Johann Kaspar Mertz
	1806–1856
Ya se asienta el Rey Ramiro from *Los Libros del Delphin*	Luys de Narváez
(*"King Ramiro is settled"*)	1490–1547
What is this noise these people make?	Simon Gorlier
	fl.1550–1584
Canarios from *Libro Quatro d' Intavolatura di Chitarroné*	Johann Hieronymus Kapsberger
	c.1580–1547
Study in G minor No. 17 from *Le Papillon*, op. 50	Mauro Giuliani
	1781–1829
Volte VI and *VII* from *A Varietie of Lute Lessons* (1610)	Robert Dowland
	1591–1641
Lady Clifton's Spirit from *A Varietie of Lute Lessons* (1610)	John Dowland
	1563–1626
Jesus bleibet meine Freude from Cantata BWV 147	Johann Sebastian Bach
(*"Jesu, Joy of Man's Desiring"*)	1685–1750
Ninna Nonna a Donegal	Giorgio Signorile
	b.1960
Prelude Saudade from *La Catedral*	Augustin Barrios Mangoré
	1885–1944

Figure 31. Ecumenical Musical Prayer Program at St. James Cathedral (Catholic), Seattle, May 1, 2020.

The performer writes in the "Notes on the Program" that follow the above list of pieces:

> The program's theme is Joy, and it falls on May Day, a day that my mother taught me to put flowers on neighbors door steps when I was a little kid, and then when I was an older kid, I heard of it being the day of solidarity among Socialists.

Musical evening prayers have been suspended in many Catholic and Protestant cathedrals in the Pacific Northwest, as in every other region of the United States and Canada, due to the pandemic. However, starting in the summer of 2022, cathedrals in Victoria, Seattle, Portland, and Greater Vancouver are slowly resuming public evening prayers with church choirs or other forms of musical performance.

Church Music Events

You can never tell if a musical event in a church is a prayer, a festival, or a concert, as some of them combine elements from more than one category, such as Ecumenical Prayer/Taizé Music/Guitar Concert at St. James Cathedral in Seattle. However, in some cases, differentiation between categories is even more difficult. These are the musical events that fall on or coincide with church holidays—Christmas, Easter, and some others, such as All Saints Day, which can last two or three days, each of which offers a musical event of a liturgical rather than extra-liturgical content.

Festivals of Church Music

In order to convey relevant information to their congregation and, moreover, to the general public, Church music festivals on the church holydays are specially advertised as such. Thus, the 2013 Feast of All Saints at St. James Church, Vancouver, BC offered High Mass on the first day and Solemn Requiem Mass and Absolution of the Dead (no dead) on the second day. The latter event, being liturgical in its order, was not such in its essence. The musical part of the event, sung and chanted from the beginning to the end, consisted of Requiem by Gabriel Fauré and medieval tunes (Plainsongs). The sequence of musical items was as follows (announced and verified by audio recording and on-site notes):

[Organ] Prelude (Adagio from Organ Symphony No. 2 by C.M. Widor)

Introit & Kyrie (*Requiem in D minor,* Op. 48 by Gabriel Fauré)

Psalm 116:1-3; 7-8 (chanted by cantor and choir)

Pie Jesu (*Requiem in D minor,* Op. 48 by Gabriel Fauré)

Offertory (*Requiem in D minor,* Op. 48 by Gabriel Fauré)

Sursum Corda & Proper Preface (chanted by cantor and choir)

Sanctus & Benedictus (*Requiem in D minor,* Op. 48 by Gabriel Fauré)

Lord's Prayer (chanted by cantor and choir)

Agnus Dei (*Requiem in D minor,* Op. 48 by Gabriel Fauré)

Organ voluntary during communion

Libera me (*Requiem in D minor,* Op. 48 by Gabriel Fauré)

Contakion (Kiev melody)

In Paradisum (*Requiem in D minor,* Op. 48 by Gabriel Fauré)

[Organ] Postlude (Nimrod from the Enigma Variations, op. 87 by Edward Elgar/Arr. by William Harris)

The varied gatherings leading up to and following Christmas are usually full of festive musical events at many churches in the area. However, they will be considered non-liturgical events and will be defined here rather as "church concerts."

Concerts in the Church

Church concerts held within the holiday framework may (and usually do) include choral music performed by a professional or amateur choir or children's choir. Among such concerts in my memory during my project in Greater Vancouver, I would note the performance of the High Spirit Choir in the Japanese Anglican church there, when the repertoire ranged from African-American spiritual style to Beatles songs. Another such group was the Emanuel Children's Choir of Richmond, British Columbia. They were quite active in various churches of the Chinese Anglican Communities of Greater Vancouver, dressed either in festive attire (Fig. 32) when they appeared in any church or in simple green T-shirts when they appeared in Emmanuel's home church.

Figure 32. Emmanuel Children's Choir performing at the Anglican Network Church of the Good Shepherd, Vancouver, BC on October 17, 2013. Photo by the author.

The Christmas concert at Emmanuel church was an event during which a children's hand chime ensemble played the tunes of popular carols, after which Emmanuel Children's Choir, all descendants of former Hong Kong families, sang various repertoire in four languages: English, Chinese, Latin, and even Hebrew.

Other types of church concerts are musical events that are not timed to coincide with church holidays or other events related to the parishioners of a particular church. Such concerts are part of the musical and educational activities in the central churches of the cities of the Pacific Northwest. Thus, the beautiful Blüthner piano, located in the Labyrinth Hall of the Trinity Episcopal Cathedral in Portland, Oregon is intended for chamber concerts in this hall. Christ Church Cathedral in Victoria, British Columbia hosts a series of concerts that combine music with an introduction to the beautiful church building. One of these concerts (recurring monthly) is called *Harps and Angels*, during which the audience takes a tour of the numerous beautiful stained-glass windows of the cathedral, leading to a small hall in which a harpist performs various pieces written for this instrument (Fig. 33).

Figure 33. "Harps and Angels" concert at Christ Church Cathedral, Victoria, BC, August 18, 2022. Photo by the author.

Not all church-related professional music groups have survived the pandemic-induced hiatus. For example, the professional choir of the Proto-Cathedral of St. James in Vancouver, Washington, which once performed a wide repertoire, seems to no longer exist.

Other Events

The people and institutions of the Pacific Northwest are sensitive to the culture of all its inhabitants, no matter where they come from. This fully applies to the church and its musical life. St. Barnabas Church in New Westminster, British Columbia is a vivid example of that. Being home to the Anglican community, most of which are descendants of Latin-American families, this church maintains rituals associated with the original location and denomination of their parishioners— Latin Catholics. Thus, the *Posada* fest and procession were held on December 15, 2013, at that church accompanied by Latin-American music. Fig. 34 presents a poster of that event.

Figure 34. Poster of the Posada fest and procession, December 15, 2013, St. Barnabas Church, New Westminster, British Columbia.

Along with welcoming Hispanic parishioners, this church embodies traditions associated with local practices, the most prominent of which is the healing circle, which is attended by people of various backgrounds. One of these events ended with a song, which was performed especially for the author by the host of the event and her niece (Fig. 35). This song was indeed an authentic song from the Cree tribe to which both women belonged. Its content was a cry for help, sung four times to the same text, accompanied by beats on the tambourine.

Figure 35. Indigenous song completing the healing circle at St. Barnabas Church, New Westminster, British Columbia, November 29, 2013. Photo by the author.

Summarizing the above reflections on music heard in churches across the Pacific Northwest, before and after the pandemic, no matter which side of the current division a church is on, we can conclude that the music in most of them, even the smallest, possesses individuality and, at the same time, unity in providing a wealth of accessible styles.

Eucharistic services are designed for different audiences—within the congregation (e.g., younger or older generation) and for the wider community. Thus, Chinese Anglican churches in Greater Vancouver (BC) hold Sunday mass twice: either in Mandarin and Cantonese or in one of them and English; Sunday mass at the Proto-Cathedral of St. James in Vancouver, Washington is held at various morning times in Latin and English; in most cathedrals, the early morning Eucharist is celebrated without music, and at the later hour, a choral Eucharistic mass. Respect for the indigenous parishioners is shown in the use of melodies associated with the music of the respective tribes.

Evening services in the main churches of large cities in the Pacific Northwest tend to include historical (modal medieval or polyphonic baroque) tunes on a regular or occasional basis. Protestant churches belonging to the evangelical division emphasize modern songs of praise, instead. On the days of church feasts and holidays, festivals of liturgical and extra-liturgical music are held in all these churches, intended rather for the general public.

Church concerts are also part of the outreach of cathedrals and major churches for the wider community. In addition to their artistic value, they often serve additional functions, such as educational or ecumenical, bringing together people from different backgrounds.

Special events in the churches of the study area are usually tailor-made, designed for a target audience, or reflect local traditions for the general public to experience. Music still plays a vital role in such events.

Chapter 6

Contribution of Modern Composers to the Church Music in the Region

Exploring hymnbooks and attending worship services in the churches of the region, one can notice that the presence of American and Canadian composers, including local residents or those born here, in the music heard in local churches, as well as the appearance of melodies composed by these creative personalities in hymnbooks, is somehow felt. This chapter will introduce the reader to the musicians who have contributed to the musical life of the church in the Pacific Northwest. We start the discussion with composers whose music is respected in the churches of the area, continuing it with a discussion of active musicians, part of whom are also residents of the area.

Neoclassics of Church Music

Healey Willan (1880–1968)

Healey Willan can be considered a true neoclassicist of the Western Church musical tradition—from its modal roots to the latest

Land, Faith, and Voice: Christian Music in the Pacific Northwest
Alexander Rosenblatt
Copyright © 2024 Jenny Stanford Publishing Pte. Ltd.
ISBN 978-981-5129-11-3 (Hardcover), 978-1-003-47332-9 (eBook)
www.jennystanford.com

polyphony. In order to understand how this composer became (and remains) probably unsurpassed in the 20th century, having really mastered the plainsong material, a small digression seems useful.

The Church of England, from its foundation to this day, has been either on the divide or in the progress of some "do/undo" action. Thus, in the late 19th century, the Millenarian movement promoted the restoration of the Jews in Palestine, thus restoring the Kingdom of Israel and setting the stage for the Second Coming and the Millennium. This movement established the Anglican Church in Jerusalem and the Middle East, converting a few local Jews and slightly more of the local Orthodox Arab Christians to Anglicanism. During the establishment of the Anglican mission in Jerusalem, a new trend came to power—the Oxford movement. This movement did not believe in the Millenarian agenda and called for the Church of England to return to its Catholic (rather than Protestant) roots. This implied, in particular, the restoration of the rich tradition of the cathedral, namely choral, music, even going deep into the layer of modal polyphony [57, pp. 32–34].

Healey Willan was born in 1880 in Balham (later part of London), England in a family of ardent supporters of the Anglo-Catholic tradition.

> When the child was two years old, the family moved to Beckenham, Kent. The Church of St George there was near the house of the family, and being of Anglo-Catholic division, influenced the boy since a plainchant has completely displaced there an Anglican chant (a musical accessory of a traditional Anglican church), so the boy was introduced to Gregorian chant from the early age and, moreover, when for the first time he heard an Anglican chant at the school, "he thought it was very funny and that the boys were having a joke" [71, pp. 4–5].

The following timeline testifies to the outstanding abilities of the young musician:

> 1891 – At age 11, plays the organ and directs the choir for services at St. Savior's Choir School;
>
> 1903 – Appointed organist and choirmaster at St. John the Baptist Church, Kensington, London, 1903–1913;
>
> 1910 – Becomes a member of the London Gregorian Association. During his years at St. John the Baptist, achieves a reputation as an authority on plainchant in the vernacular;

1913 – Moves to Canada to become head of the theory department of the Toronto Conservatory of Music and remains associated with the Conservatory 1913–1936 [72, pp. 14–15].

The story of Willan's move to Canada has a slightly mystical connotation. Just like his contemporary, the composer A. Schoenberg (1874–1951) who was truly afraid of the number 13, Willan attached great importance to the numbers 3 and 13 in his life, perhaps without a hint of fear. The Canadian Encyclopedia reads:

In 1913 Willan received an invitation from A. S. Vogt, principal of the Toronto Conservatory of Music (TCM, later Royal Conservatory of Music), offering him the position of head of the theory department, to succeed Humfrey Anger. A friend of Vogt had recommended Willan after hearing him play in London. Years later Willan said that the numbers 3 and 13 had played an important part in his life and, since the invitation arrived on the third day of the third month in 1913 when Willan was 33, he decided to accept it; however, though Celtic mysticism (inherited or assumed) was an important element in his personality, it is likely that the decision was based more on economic necessity than on numerology. Three weeks after his arrival in Toronto he accepted the post of organist-choirmaster at St. Paul's Anglican Church, Bloor Street [73, "The Canadian Years" section].

Whatever the story, having arrived in Toronto and received a job, the composer remained there until the end of his very fruitful creative life. After a few years at St. Paul's Anglican Church, Willan became the organist and musical director of St. Mary Magdalene Church in Toronto, with which his professional life is further connected. Here the composer established two choirs, which became his "laboratory" for both modal and polyphonic compositions.

Given the Church of England's ban on Latin texts, inevitably associated with Gregorian chants, Willan's contribution to Anglican music and at the same time the cornerstone of his creative style is the combination of plainchant and English text. His liturgical music always possesses a modal flavor, be it monody, four-part polyphony, or adaptation of a modal harmony to historical tunes of the early Anglican tradition—those by John Merbecke (1503–1578) or tunes adopted from the Roman Catholic liturgy (with English text), such as *Veni Emmanuel* (Example 7).

Example 7. *Veni Emmanuel,* arranged by H. Willan, as appears in *The Book of Common Praise,* 1938, p. 58.

The Book of Common Praise, 1938 [61] lists 18 of Willan's arrangements of Plainchants and Merbecke's melodies, whereas *The Hymn Book of the Anglican Church of Canada and United Church of Canada,* 1971 [56] lists 19 such arrangements. The former edition considers Willan "not only an outstanding composer of church music but also an authority on accompaniments for plainsong melodies" [61, p. iv].

With the further development of his musical style, Healey Willan (Fig. 36) created a number of works for a four-part choir, which still retain the features of modal texture and harmony. Such, in particular, are the *Great O Antiphons.*

Figure 36.   Healey Willan in his studio. Credit: Mary Willan.

Written in 1957, the seven *Great O Antiphons of Advent* are so named because they all begin with the capital "O." Associated with the seven days before Christmas, each antiphon takes as its theme one of the names (or attributes) of Christ, while their combined texts were later paraphrased in the hymn "O come, O come, Emmanuel." Willan's settings share common musical solutions but each is slightly different reflecting the individual text. *O Emmanuel* (Example 8) is the last of the Great O Antiphons characterized by two types of polyphony: choral-modal (bars 1–12) and canonical (from bar 13 onwards) four-part texture.

The only audio recording of Willan's *O Emmanuel* available on YouTube is a live recording from Advent Carols & Lessons service (2002) sung by Vancouver's Christ Church Cathedral Choir directed by Rupert Lang.

Example 8. *O Emmanuel*, as appears in Healey Willan and Carl Schalk, *The Great O Antiphons of Advent*, St. Louis, MO: Concordia Publishing House, 1985, p. 15.

O Emmanuel
December 23

HEALEY WILLAN
Revised by CARL SCHALK

Modal harmony is also characteristic of Willan's organ works, giving them a recognizable style. Such are his *Prelude & Fughetta* from his *Five Pieces* written in 1959 for Gerald Wheeler for the organ dedication at St. Matthew's Church in Ottawa, ON. The harmonic progressions in the Prelude (Example 9) are superficially reminiscent of Bach's organ works, but Willan's return to modal harmony from chromatic tonality is not one and the same as Bach's chromatic tonality, which grew out of linear polyphony.

Example 9. *Prelude,* bars 1–8, as appear in Healey Willan, *Five Pieces for Organ*, Toronto: BMI Canada Ltd., p. 6.

All of Willan's academic degrees were honorary ones, at a later age, for his contribution to the Anglican musical tradition. The highest sign of his recognition was the writing of the homage anthem, *O Lord Our Governour*, commissioned to him for the Coronation of Queen Elizabeth II, performed at Westminster Abbey on June 2, 1953, with the composer present.

Patrick Wedd (1948–2019)

While Canadian hymnals from the late 1930s to early 1970s credited Healey Willan for his proficiency in plainchant and modal harmony on par with another British-born composer Ralph Vaughan Williams (1872–1958), whose arrangements of medieval melodies were part of any English, American, or Canadian hymnbook and date of birth was the same as Willan's—October 12, later hymnbooks such as *Common Praise*, 1998 consider Patrick Wedd as a key figure in the development of the musical style of the updated hymnbooks [74].

Patrick Wedd (Fig. 37) was born in Simcoe, Ontario, Canada in 1948. He began organ studies at age 11, while at the age of 12, he was already serving as organist-choirmaster at St. Paul's Church in Port Robinson, ON.

Figure 37.   Patrick Wedd. Credit: Katrina Bertrand.

Upon receiving a master's degree in music from Trinity College at the University of Toronto, Patrick Wedd moved to Vancouver, British Columbia in 1970, where he took a position as organist-choirmaster at St. Mary's Anglican Church and, five years later, a similar position at Christ Church Cathedral where he worked for another 11 years. Since 1986, Wedd has lived and worked in Montreal, Quebec. There he served as artistic director of the Tudor Singers Mixed Choir and music director of St. Andrew and St. Paul Church. In 1987, he became a member of the editorial team that would develop the *Common Praise* hymnbook to be released in 1998. From 1993 until his retirement in 2018, Wedd served as music director at Christ Church Cathedral in Montreal.

In terms of musical style, Patrick Wedd (unlike Healey Willan) is not a proponent of pure medieval modality but rather uses the sonority of white key clusters (i.e. diatonic) rather than following the logic of modal sequences. Such are the many of Wedd's multiple-voice settings and accessories that appear in the abovementioned hymnbook, such as *Glory to You* (Example 10) accompanied by handbells.

Example 10. Patrick Wedd. *Glory to You*, Common Praise (1998), No. 740.

Another of Wedd's contributions to the North American church music is using the syncope patterns in "modern style" melodies that follow the trends of the song style of the early 1960s on which the composer grew up when he was a teen. The syncopated style of Wedd's hymns is one of the typical features in his songlike hymns (as against settings), such as *Lion and Lamb Lying Together* (Example 11).

The musician's death shortly after his retirement shocked the Anglicans in the cathedral. In a Facebook post, Bishop Mary Irwin-Gibson called Wedd "a wonderful musician and composer who gave his heart and soul to serve the One who gave him these gifts" [74].

Example 11. *Lion and Lamb Lying Together* (bars 1-4), Common Praise, No. 597.

Active Musicians and Hymnwriters

Rupert Lang

After Patrick Wedd left Vancouver for Montreal in 1986, his position in the Christ Church Cathedral was offered to Rupert Lang, a young musician who worked then in one of the Anglican churches in West Vancouver.

Rupert Lang (Fig. 38), who comes from a family of an Anglican priest, spent years studying organ and church music in England, at such respected institutions as the Royal School of Church Music, the Royal College of Organists, and finally the University of Cambridge, where he received a master's degree.

Figure 38.   Rupert Lang. Courtesy of Christ Church Cathedral, Vancouver, BC.

From the very beginning in the cathedral, Lang was faced with the great changes introduced then to the liturgical life of the congregation by combining two morning services (9:30 am and 11:15 am) into one service at 10:30 am. The meaning of these changes was that "[t]he two liturgies had very different musical styles and Rupert was charged with finding settings that might appeal to those who loved traditional music and those who loved contemporary song. Of course, he did this by writing something new altogether, the mass setting *Terra Nova* [...] to bring these worlds together," stated Rev. Peter Elliott, Dean and rector of Christ Church Cathedral. "Even 20+ years later, to my ears, it sounds fresh and still intrigues listeners with its combination of melody and electronic music" [75].

As is historically accustomed for the position of organist and choirmaster/church music director, Rupert Land applied his talent to minister his audience as a composer, cathedral organ player, and church choir director and conductor. Among his many compositions, *Mass for Many Nations* (1994) deserves special attention.

The mass was commissioned by the cathedral, with the belief that *everyone* is welcome in this place. Weaving this philosophy into a mass setting, Lang has set each movement to reflect a particular aspect or group of the world community, from the Lord's Prayer *Yamman, Yabban*, representing the influence of Aramaic on the Hebrew Bible, to the presentation of a local, indigenous melody. Such is *Affirmation of Faith*, adapted from a Prayer Song by Chief Dan George (Example 12). The melody of this song is filled with the fragrance and images of naivety and the coastal landscape. It is accompanied by a piano that provides clarity, simplicity, and transparency, following the pattern of *world music* interpreting a local melody. At least, this is how this melody is perceived during the performance in the cathedral.

Example 12. Rupert Lang. *Affirmation of Faith* from Mass for Many Nations, as printed in a Sunday Mass booklet, November 24, 2013, Christ Church Cathedral, Vancouver, BC, Canada.

Cantor 1   I believe in God,

Creator of the Universe.   *repeat all*

dwelling for-e-ver beyond time and space.

Cantor 2   I believe in Jesus Christ who came to live amongst us

and let us see what God is like.   *repeat all*

Cantor 3   and I believe in the Holy Spirit sent from God through Jesus

to be our guide and comforter.   *repeat all*

Cantors   Therefore, I believe in love, in hope, compassion, joy and faith,

and forgiveness   and e-ter-nal life.   *repeat all*

words: Frances Somerville
Music: Rupert Lang, adapted freely from a Prayer Song by Chief Dan George

In 2021, the Vancouver School of Theology awarded the musician an Honorary Doctor of Divinity for his contribution to the integration of theology and ministry practice, as well as ecumenical dialogue. Concluding the event, Rev. Peter Elliott said:

> Not since Healey Willan has Canada known such a prolific composer of church music nor a church musician whose work is so widely appreciated. Bridging two centuries, Rupert's compositions possess the unusual quality of being very rooted in their time yet transcending that to join with the classical treasures of the Anglican choral repertoire. As a Cathedral Director of Music and Organist, he combines a deep sense of pastoral care with liturgical sensitivity. In every way, his ministry as a church musician is outstanding [76].

Bob Hurd

On the American side of the Pacific Northwest, the most characteristic events in terms of music take place in Catholic churches and in the music of composers, represented, in particular, in Catholic hymnals. One of the composers representing contemporary trends in Western Church music is Bob Hurd, himself a resident of the Pacific Northwest. "With more than 45 years of composing under his belt, Bob Hurd knows a thing or two about music and liturgy. That might explain why so many of his songs for worship have become classics in the repertoire" [77].

Figure 39.   Bob Hurd. Credit: Oregon Catholic Press.

Bob Hurd (Fig. 39) began composing music shortly after Vatican II when the need arose for new music in the local language, music that could be sung by the whole assembly. Following this trend (or rather, the request), Hurd pioneered bilingual music, in which compositions were based on complementary English and Spanish texts. Thus, one of his latest cycles, *The Bread of Your Word*, includes eight songs for Advent, Lent, Holy Thursday, the Easter season, and Ordinary Time, as well as the complete *Santa Clara Mass*.

Choral and Melody editions of *Worship IV* include Hurd's bilingual song *Pan de Vita* [bread of life]. The Melody edition features Bob Hurd's original (monophonic) melody, in which the sequence-based melody explicitly alludes to the harmony of classic Western tonality (Example 13a). The choral edition contains a three-part polyphony for refrain and a two-voice version for verses, all arranged by Craig Kingsbury. The refrain here is designed for a soprano-alto-tenor texture, without a bass line (which is clearly discernible in the monophonic version), thereby blurring the tonal basis of this melody and making it less songlike (Example 13b).

Example 13.   Bob Hurd. *Pan de Vita*, Worship IV, No. 925 (Refrain)

(a) as presented in the Melody edition.

925 Pan de Vida

(b) as presented in the Choral edition.

Sally Ann Morris

The most published living composer in American hymnbooks, Sally Ann Morris (Fig. 40) is a songwriter focused on church hymns and praise songs.

Figure 40.   Sally Ann Morris. Credit: Wake Forest University School of Divinity, Winston-Salem, NC.

Sally Ann Morris was born, lives, and works in North Carolina. Most of her tunes published in *Worship IV* are unaccompanied melodies (even in a choral edition), such as *If Christ Had Not Been Raised from Death* (Example 14). They all clearly display the tonal thinking of the composer. One clearly hears the harmony of regular Western tonality behind simple melodies that use diatonic sequences and even *natural seventh*, however, you feel it is not a modal tune, and you easily can remember it! Yet, a strictly formal look to these tunes still cannot attribute them to the legacy of pure church music, nor do they belong to any medieval tradition.

The composer, who is affiliated with Presbyterian Church (USA), since the early 1990s found herself writing songs acceptable to modern congregations of both Protestant and Catholic churches [78], being suitable to congregational singing, monophonic, and with no high seventh in minor keys. This is why songs, hymns, and settings by Sally Ann Morris are part of many hymnbooks of the early 21st century that belong to any of the contemporary Western churches in North America.

Example 14. Sally Ann Morris. *If Christ Had Not Been Raised from Death,* Worship IV, No. 497 (bars 1–8).

497 If Christ Had Not Been Raised from Death

Looking at the styles of the composers discussed in the chapter and the gradual change in the style of the church music during just several decades, one may assume that music style in Western churches of North America in general, and the Pacific Northwest, in particular, repeats the way of Western music during centuries: from modal monophony through polyphony to homophony and tonality. Thus, reconstruction of a pure plainchant style performed by H. Willan, his own examples of modal polyphony and modal harmony to the historical tunes were succeeded by white-keys based clusters that just formally followed the "scales" of medieval church modes being rather sonority patterns.

At certain steps, all this was shadowed by the rhythmic patterns of the secular songs of the 1960s. A tribute to vernacular languages in church hymns was the next step where the music style was rather matching the target audience than following a certain pattern. Finally (as of today), unaccompanied melodies came back to church music, in which however, regular harmony of the contemporary song is clearly heard, not being sung or played. Composers chosen to represent this change of styles were either residents of the region or those whose music influences modern-day church service in the Pacific Northwest.

Concluding Thoughts

We have been standing at the car rental counter at SeaTac International Airport in Seattle for two hours now, waiting for a mid-size car ordered months ago. Friendly smiling office worker raises her hands: We have no mid-size cars available. Please go to the garage and choose another size for the same price! We follow the proposal, going down to the Hertz garage to see a few economy cars and entire rows of full-size cars. After a brief discussion with my son, we choose a silver Nissan Altima and, having completed the formalities, find ourselves the owners (for four days) of a comfortable, powerful, and according to the concepts of yesterday, even quite economical car. Americans have already abandoned the concept of a big car anytime, everywhere, and switched to smaller cars, so, having initially ordered a mid-size auto, in the end, we had no choice but to feel like Americans of past decades, overcoming miles of federal highways in a big vehicle.

Among the most vivid things that have remained in my memory from numerous trips around the region and meetings with people, two such events deserve mention at the end of this story. The first was the response of an Anglican missionary bishop, whom I asked (at the very beginning of the split) if it seemed to him that their flagship had been wrecked. The clergymen thought for a moment, then said: "You are the second person to tell me this."—"So who was the first?" I wondered, and he replied, "Jesus, in a dream. Since then I have become a missionary." The second time was when I, an Israeli researcher, was asked by a minister of a small Anglican church at UBC to give a lecture on church music in Jerusalem to his parishioners from the pulpit. When I agreed, he noticed that a *rabbi-in-residence* at the Anglican Cathedral was lecturing to the parishioners on the condition that he did not stand in the place of the preacher. I said that it would be a great honor for me to stay there. Then the priest, Rev. Harold Munn, said, "You and me are the same," meaning that we are both human, and the rest is just conventions. This phrase has since symbolized for me the openness of people in the places I have visited and explored.

The in situ part of my project is complete, and we are moving on to the "ethnography" of my son, who is interested in visiting, where allowed, or at least see the headquarters and facilities of high-tech giants—Apple, Intel, Google, and others, all of which are located in the iconic Silicon Valley, specifically in San Jose, which, contrary to popular belief, is not a suburb of San Francisco, but a separate city with, which is important for guests, very friendly conditions for free street parking.

Arriving at San Francisco International Airport, we are faced with exactly the same situation at the car rental agency: There are no mid-size cars. This time around, after a longer discussion than in Seattle (because there are more full-size cars to choose from) and determined that if so, then we feel like Americans to the end and take a large American-made car. First, we decide to grab a brand new red Dodge Charger but a heavily spring-loaded button on the gearshift lever challenges our preferences, as I have issues with lateral thumb pressure on my right hand, and my son is still 18, so he is not eligible to drive a rental car. What a pity! Without leaving the thought of "being in America like an American," we get into a dark blue turbocharged Chevy Malibu and continue our "American experience" until the end of our journey.

Concluding the material and ideas summarized and expressed in the book, I would like to note that music turned out to be the very means by which I got acquainted with the history, culture, and social phenomena of the region. Considering that along with this long-term project I carried out another such project exploring music of various churches in the Holy Land, namely in Israel, various historical and cultural parallels became a useful vehicle to develop the point of view, by which the things were presented in the book.

Zooming out from the material into the global perspective, it seems that differences between customs, street food brands, and even popular car sizes have become closer between continents over the past decade, people have become more open and, in fact, more open-minded than it was before the era of total and global availability of social networks, the Internet and, very importantly, translation services. Nevertheless, the very fact of various divisions and divides remains probably one of the traits that a person possesses and which is difficult to give up. This still leaves us open to further exploration of the development of cultures, including those discussed in the book.

I wonder if in another 10 or 15 years there still will be a split within the Protestant churches and two different approaches to the musical part of worship in the Catholic churches of the Pacific Northwest. It is doubtful that this will be the case. Thus, my (or any other researcher's) visit to the area during the 2030s may bring many new and interesting details about the development of church music in the area and other related social, cultural, and artistic palettes.

References

[1] A. Appadurai, *Modernity at Large: Cultural Dimensions of Globalization.* Minneapolis: University of Minnesota Press, 1996.

[2] T. Browner, Ed., *Music of the First Nations: Tradition and Innovation in Native North America.* Urbana: University of Illinois Press, 2009.

[3] H. S. Donaldson, "Toward a Musical Praxis of Justice: A Survey of Global and Indigenous Canadian Song in the Hymnals of the Anglican, Presbyterian, and United Churches of Canada through Their History." *The Hymn,* vol. 63, no. 2, pp. 18–26, Spring 2012.

[4] K. E. Perry, *Heritage Churches of the Indigenous Peoples of British Columbia: Historical Events & Architectural Elements of Church Structures.* Surrey, BC: Hancock House, 2019.

[5] M. Bruce-Mitford, *Signs & Symbols: An Illustrated Guide to Their Origins and Meanings.* London: Dorling Kindersley, 2019.

[6] K. Nerburn, Ed., *The Wisdom of the Native Americans.* Novato, CA: New World Library, 1999.

[7] V. Strauss, "Christopher Columbus: 3 things you think he did that he didn't," *The Washington Post,* Oct. 14, 2013. [Online]. Available: https://www.washingtonpost.com/news/answer-sheet/wp/2013/10/14/christopher-columbus-3-things-you-think-he-did-that-he-didnt. [Accessed: Jan. 28, 2022].

[8] J. M. McMullen, *The History of Canada: From Its First Discovery to the Present Time.* Brockville, C.W.: J. M'Mullen, 1855.

[9] J. P. Dunn, "The Mission to the Ouabache," *Indiana Historical Society Publications,* vol. 3, no. 4, Indianapolis, IN: The Bowen–Merrill Company, 1902.

[10] T. A. Surovell, "Simulating Coastal Migration in New World Colonization." *Current Anthropology,* vol. 44, no. 4, pp. 580–591, Aug. 2003.

[11] *Captain Cook Society,* FAQ. [Online]. Available: https://www.captaincooksociety.com/home/captain-cook-society/faq. [Accessed: Jan 29, 2022].

[12] C. Davis and W. K. Lamb, *Greater Vancouver Book: An Urban Encyclopedia*. Surrey, BC: Linkman Press, 1997.

[13] M. Francis, "Vancouver – Coevorden," Portal of the Municipality of Coevorden. [Online]. Available: *Gemeente Coevorden*, https://geschiedeniscoevorden.nl/coevorden/picardtreeks/vancouver-coevorden. [Accessed: Feb 12, 2022].

[14] R. Fulford, *The Prince Consort*. London: Macmillan, 1949.

[15] B. McGillivray, "Victoria, British Columbia, Canada," *Britannica*. [Online]. Available: https://www.britannica.com/place/Victoria-British-Columbia. [Accessed Feb 18, 2022].

[16] "George Washington – Facts, Presidency & Quotes," *Biography*. [Online]. Available: https://www.biography.com/us-president/george-washington [Accessed Feb 21, 2022].

[17] D. M. Buerge, "Chief Seattle and Chief Joseph: From Indians to Icons," *University of Washington Libraries Digital Collections*. [Online]. Available: https://content.lib.washington.edu/aipnw/buerge2.html. [Accessed Feb 24, 2022].

[18] G. Vancouver and J. Vancouver, *A Voyage of Discovery to the North Pacific Ocean, and Round the World*. London: J. Stockdale, 1801.

[19] A. C. Magnuson, *In Search of the Schooner Exact*. [Online]. Available: http://www.craigmagnuson.com/exact.htm. [Accessed Jan 28, 2022].

[20] P. Olsen, *Portland in the 1960s: Stories from the Counterculture*. Charleston, SC: The History Press, 2012.

[21] G. Martin, "The Naming of British Columbia," *Albion: A Quarterly Journal Concerned with British Studies*, vol. 10, no. 3, pp. 257–263, 1978.

[22] G. P. V. Akrigg and H. B. Akrigg, *British Columbia Chronicle, 1847–1871: Gold and Colonists*. Vancouver, BC: Discovery Press, 1977.

[23] L. Ishiguro, *Nothing to Write Home About: British Family Correspondence and the Settler Colonial Everyday in British Columbia*. Vancouver, BC: UBC Press, 2019.

[24] W. J. Brier, "How Washington Territory Got Its Name," *The Pacific Northwest Quarterly*, vol. 51, no. 1, pp. 13–15, 1960.

[25] E. E. Bush, "Dear D. C., you can't call yourself 'State of Washington'. That's our name," *The Seattle Times*. October 19, 2016. [Online]. Available: https://www.seattletimes.com/nation-world/dear-dc-you-cant-call-yourself-state-of-washington-thats-our-name [Accessed Apr. 17, 2022].

[26] J. Marschner, *Oregon 1859: A Snapshot in Time*, Portland, OR: Timber Press, 2008, p. 187.

[27] J. R. Jewell, "Thwarting Southern schemes and British bluster in the Pacific Northwest," in *Civil War Wests: Testing the Limits of the United States*, A. Arenson, Ed. Berkeley: University of California Press, 2015, pp. 15–32.

[28] B. A. Kosmin and A. Keysar, *American Religious Identification Survey (ARIS 2008)*. Hartford, CT: Trinity College, 2009. [Online]. Available: https://livinginliminality.files.wordpress.com/2009/03/aris_report_2008.pdf. [Accessed: Jun. 5, 2022].

[29] "Religious affiliation of Canadian residents of British Columbia in 2011," *Statista*. [Online]. Available: https://www.statista.com/statistics/534302/religious-affiliation-of-canadian-residents-of-british-columbia/ [Accessed: Jun. 5, 2022].

[30] M. Silk, "The Pacific Northwest is the American religious future," *Religion News Service*. May 31, 2019. [Online]. Available: https://religionnews.com/2019/05/31/the-pacific-northwest-is-the-american-religious-future/ [Accessed: Jun. 11, 2022].

[31] R. E. Luker, "Churches, Mainstream," in *Encyclopedia.com*. [Online]. Available: https://www.encyclopedia.com/defense/energy-government-and-defense-magazines/churches-mainstream. [Accessed: Jul. 1, 2022].

[32] W. Herberg, *Protestant–Catholic–Jew: An Essay in American Religious Sociology*. Chicago: The University of Chicago Press, 1955.

[33] J. Brooks, "Explaining polygamy and its history in the Mormon Church," *The Conversation*, Aug. 18, 2017. [Online]. Available: https://theconversation.com/explaining-polygamy-and-its-history-in-the-mormon-church-81384. [Accessed: Jul. 4, 2022].

[34] D. Taranowski, "The Mainline Seven Sisters," *INFO First Congregational Church in Melrose*, Feb. 11, 2020. [Online]. Available: https://fccmelrose.org/2020/02/11/the-mainline-seven-sisters/. [Accessed: Jan. 20, 2022].

[35] J. Jenkins, "Survey: White mainline Protestants outnumber white evangelicals, while 'nones' shrink," *Religion News Service*. Jul. 8, 2021. [Online]. Available: https://religionnews.com/2021/07/08/survey-white-mainline-protestants-outnumber-white-evangelicals/. [Accessed: Jul. 8, 2022].

[36] *Religious Landscape Study*, Pew Research Center, Washington, D.C. (2014). [Online]. Available: https://www.pewresearch.org/religion/religious-landscape-study/. [Accessed: Jul. 8, 2022].

[37] B. Bethune and P. Treble, "The key to growing Protestant churches," *Maclean's*, Nov. 16, 2016. [Online]. Available: https://www.macleans.ca/society/it-has-risen-is-this-the-key-to-growing-protestant-churches/. [Accessed Jul 8, 2022].

[38] A. Stewart, "'Gone by 2040': Why some religions are declining in Canada faster than ever," *Global News*, Jan. 8, 2022. [Online]. Available: https://globalnews.ca/news/8471086/religion-decline-canada/. [Accessed Jul. 8, 2022].

[39] *Indian Residential Schools*, The UBC Indian Residential School History and Dialogue Centre (2020). [Online]. Available: https://irshdc.ubc.ca/learn/indian-residential-schools/. [Accessed: Jul. 8, 2022].

[40] W. Dickson, "Missionary Work and Indian Policy." A letter of William Dickson to his children, *1834. Digital History*, ID 241, University of Huston, 2021. [Online]. Available: https://www.digitalhistory.uh.edu/disp_textbook.cfm?smtID=3&psid=241. [Accessed: Jul. 9, 2022].

[41] R. H. Ruby and J. A. Brown, *John Slocum and the Indian Shaker Church*. Norman: University of Oklahoma Press, 1996.

[42] "Shakers" (revised and updated by A. Augustyn), *Britannica*. [Online]. Available: https://www.britannica.com/topic/Shakers. [Accessed Jul. 9, 2022].

[43] *Seeing a New Day: A 150 Year History of St. Peter Catholic Mission*. Suquamish, WA: Port Madison Indian Reservation, 2012.

[44] M. Bruce-Mitford, *Signs & Symbols: An Illustrated Guide to Their Origins and Meanings*. London: Dorling Kindersley, 2019.

[45] *Worship II. A Hymnal for Roman Catholic Parishes*. Chicago, IL: G.I.A. Publications, 1975.

[46] *Anglican Church of Canada: Anglican Council of Indigenous Peoples*. [Online]. Available: https://www.anglican.ca/about/ccc/acip/ [Accessed Sen. 17, 2022].

[47] E. N. Wright, *The Indian Shaker Church: Colonialism, Continuity, and Resistance, 1882–1920*. A thesis submitted in fulfillment of the requirements for the degree of Master of Arts. Vancouver: The University of British Columbia, 2013.

[48] R. B. Inverarity, *Art of the Northwest Coast Indians*. Berkely: University of California Press, 1950.

[49] *The Canadian Conference of Catholic Bishops*, "Indigenous Art Collection." [Online]. Available: https://www.cccb.ca/indigenous-peoples/resources/cccb-art-collection/. [Accessed Oct. 1, 2022].

[50] *Seattle Art Museum*, "Paradise Series #1: Eve with Fish and Snake." [Online]. Available: https://art.seattleartmuseum.org/objects/9942/paradise-series-1-eve-with-fish-and-snake?ctx=69bb53e2-f0a9-4e6f-a9a3-8e0e666f8c6a&idx=66. [Accessed Oct. 1, 2022].

[51] S. Diamond, *Pacific Northwest Indigenous Art Activity Book*, Vancouver, BC: Native Northwest, 2021.

[52] A. Rosenblatt, "Musical Cultures in the National Hymnbooks of the 1990s." *Min-Ad: Israel Studies in Musicology Online*, vol. 14, pp. 24–36, 2018.

[53] *Tra Le Sollecitudini*, Instruction on Sacred Music by Pope Pius X, 22 November 1903, [Online]. Available: https://adoremus.org/1903/11/22/tra-le-sollecitudini. [Accessed January 22, 2019].

[54] *The New English Hymnal* (Full Musical Edition). Norwich: Canterbury Press, 1994.

[55] A. Fortesque, "Mass, Ceremony of the," in *The Catholic encyclopedia*, C. G. Herbermann et al., Eds., vol. 9. New York: The Encyclopedia Press, 1913, pp. 799–800.

[56] *The Hymn Book* (The Hymn Book of the Anglican Church of Canada and United Church of Canada), Toronto: Southam-Murray, 1971.

[57] A. Rosenblatt, *Music of the Contemporary Arab-Anglican Churches in Israel*. Thesis submitted for the degree of "Doctor of Philosophy," The Hebrew University of Jerusalem, 2012.

[58] F. Blume, *Protestant Church Music: A History*. New York: W. W. Norton, 1974.

[59] I. Jones and P. Webster, "Anglican 'Establishment' Reactions to 'Pop' Church Music in England, 1956–c.1990," *Studies in Church History*, vol. 42, pp. 429–441, 2006.

[60] F. R. C. Clarke, "Some musical aspects of The Hymn Book, 1971," in *Sing Out the Glad News: Hymn Tunes in Canada* (Proceedings of the conference held in Toronto February 7 and 8, 1986), John Beckwith, Ed. Toronto: University of Toronto Press, 1987, pp. 149–155.

[61] *The Book of Common Praise* (Being the Hymn Book of the Church of England in Canada). Toronto: Humphrey Milford, 1938.

[62] *Worship. A Hymnal and Service Book for Roman Catholics,* Third Edition. Chicago, IL: G.I.A. Publications, 1986.

[63] *Worship,* Fourth Edition. Chicago, IL: G.I.A. Publications, 2011.

[64] *The Adoremus Hymnal*, Second Edition. San Francisco, CA: Ignatus Press, 2011.

[65] *Common Praise* (Anglican Church of Canada). Toronto: Anglican Book Centre, 1998.

[66] *Hymns of Universal Praise* (Bilingual Edition). Hong Kong: Chinese Christian Literature Council Ltd., 1996.

[67] *The Hymnal* (According to the Use of the Episcopal Church). New York: The Church Hymnal Corporation, 1940.

[68] *The Hymnal* (According to the Use of the Episcopal Church). New York: The Church Hymnal Corporation, 1982.

[69] *St. James' High Mass Choir.* [Online]. Available: https://stjames.bc.ca/choir. [Accessed March 19, 2023].

[70] *Trinity Episcopal Cathedral*, "Trinity Music" page. [Online]. Available: https://www.trinity-episcopal.org/trinity-music. [Accessed April 10, 2023].

[71] F. R. C. Clarke, *Healey Willan: Life and Music.* Toronto: University of Toronto Press, 1983.

[72] G. Bryant, *Healey Willan Catalogue.* Ottawa: National Library of Canada, 1972.

[73] G. Bryant and T. C. Brown, "Healey Willan," *The Canadian Encyclopedia.* [Online]. Available: https://www.thecanadianencyclopedia.ca/en/article/healey-willan-emc. [Accessed May 20, 2023].

[74] M. Puddister, "Remembering Patrick Wedd: Celebrated church musician was 'a force of nature'." *Anglican Journal*, June 3, 2019. [Online]. Available: https://anglicanjournal.com/remembering-patrick-wedd-celebrated-church-musician-was-a-force-of-nature. [Accessed May 24, 2023].

[75] P. Elliott, "A Celebration of Rupert Lang's 30th Anniversary," *Diocese of New Westminster (Anglican Church of Canada).* [Online]. Available: https://www.vancouver.anglican.ca/news/a-celebration-of-rupert-langs-30th-anniversary. [Accessed May 26, 2023].

[76] "VST Announces 2021 Honorary Doctor of Divinity Recipient," *The Vancouver School of Theology.* [Online]. Available: https://vst.edu/2020/12/10/vst-announces-2021-honorary-doctor-of-divinity-recipient. [Accessed May 26, 2023].

[77] "Bob Hurd," *Oregon Catholic Press.* [Online]. Available: https://www.ocp.org/en-us/artists/137/bob-hurd. [Accessed May 25, 2023].

[78] "Sally Ann Morris," *GIA Publications, Ltd.* [Online]. Available: https://www.giamusic.com/bios/morris_sally_ann.cfm. [Accessed May 27, 2023].

Index

For Product Safety Concerns and Information please contact our EU
representative GPSR@taylorandfrancis.com
Taylor & Francis Verlag GmbH, Kaufingerstraße 24, 80331 München, Germany

9 789815 129113